Roger Zelazny

Twayne's United States Authors Series

Frank Day, Editor
Clemson University

TUSAS 640

Roger Zelazny. Photo by Beth Gwynn.

Roger Zelazny

Jane M. Lindskold

Lynchburg College

Twayne Publishers ■ New York

Maxwell Macmillan Canada ■ Toronto

Maxwell Macmillan International ■ New York Oxford Singapore Sydney

Roger Zelazny
Jane M. Lindskold

Copyright 1993 by Twayne Publishers

Twayne Publishers   Maxwell Macmillan Canada, Inc.
Macmillan Publishing Company 1200 Eglinton Avenue East
866 Third Avenue   Suite 200
New York, New York 10022   Don Mills, Ontario M3C 3N1

Library of Congress Cataloging-in-Publication Data

Lindskold, Jane M.
    Roger Zelazny / Jane M. Lindskold.
    p.   cm. – (Twayne's United States authors series; TUSAS 640)
    Includes bibliographical references and index.
    ISBN 0-8057-3953-X
    1. Zelazny, Roger – Criticism and interpretation. 2. Science
fiction, American – History and criticism I. Title. II. Series.
PS3576.E43Z76 1993
813'.54 – dc20   93-29505
                                                                              CIP

The paper used in this publication meets the minimum
requirements of American National Standard for Information
Sciences – Permanence of Paper for Printed Library Materials,
ANSI Z39.48-1984.

10 9 8 7 6 5 4 3 2 1

Printed in the United States of America.

For my parents,
John Eric Lindskold and Barbara DiSalle Lindskold,
in grateful acknowledgment of their continual support and love

Contents

Preface

If I were to go back to first causes, this book has its origin in conversations with my former roommate (and still close friend) Kathy Curran on the fascinating contradictions in Roger Zelazny's Amber novels. We would take a break from our homework (hers in biology, mine in English) to try and figure out which character's version of events was the most accurate. The Amber books were ideal for speculation, since no one ever tells the full truth to anyone – not even Corwin to himself. Kathy also made her collection of Zelazny novels available to me; I still vividly remember finishing *Eye of Cat* and putting it back into our milk crate shelves and thinking, "This guy is weird!"

A more immediate cause for this book comes from a chance question asked me by Russell Christian, a very fine gentleman who worked in Fordham's Duane Library. Russ knew of my enthusiasm for science fiction and asked me which science fiction author I would pick as my favorite. After much pondering, I chose Zelazny. When Russ asked me the reasons for my choice, I answered that Zelazny's pieces had such a wide variety of moods and themes that his work never bored me. In fact, I hadn't realized that the same guy who wrote the Amber novels also wrote *Lord of Light* until alphabetical shelving drew it to my attention.

Having acknowledged my preference, I eventually sent the only fan letter I have ever written. I dropped it in the mail, deleted the text from my files, and never expected to get an answer. I was surprised – almost shocked – to get a postcard in return. Pleased, I wrote a brief letter back and with that letter started a correspondence that has continued steadily to the present day.

Whether that correspondence would have taken off the way it has if I had never met Zelazny is anyone's guess. Through my friend Chuck Gannon, I learned that Zelazny would be the guest of honor at Lunacon in Tarrytown, New York, in March 1989. I had never been to a science fiction convention, but I decided to go and take a look at this person with whom I had been trading short letters for the past six months.

Intimidated by the crowds of people thronging Zelazny with their shopping bags of books, I almost didn't introduce myself. Encouraged by a very nice book dealer who assured me (from his greater knowledge of science fiction conventions) that meeting fans was what the writers were there for, I joined the crowd.

When my turn came, Zelazny turned, glanced at my hands as if looking for the book or program he was to sign, and then looked at me. I stuttered, "Mr. Zelazny" (mispronouncing the name), "I'm Jane Lindskold." He smiled and grasped my hand, saying, "You came!"

His delight was so genuine that I overcame my immediate impulse to say a few words and then retreat. Instead, I accepted his invitation to sit and chat in between autographs. There I also had the pleasure of meeting Ted Krulik, whose 1986 biography of Zelazny I had read.

During that Lunacon, I had two opportunities to talk with Zelazny. In the course of going over some questions I had for an article I was writing ("All Roads *Do* Lead to Amber"), we discovered that we shared a large number of interests. When Lunacon was over, this conversation continued through our correspondence, filling letters that sometimes exceeded 20 pages apiece.

Selections from that correspondence make up a large portion of the source material in this book. If the sentences are sometimes choppy or littered with abbreviations, the reason is that these letters were never written with publication in mind, only as a long conversation through the post. My sincere thanks go to Zelazny for permitting me such extensive use of this material.

Lunacon would be our only meeting until April 1990, when Zelazny accepted an invitation to come to Lynchburg College, where I had begun teaching, as a Thornton writer. This visit was in a calmer setting than our first, and we took advantage of it to talk at length.

That same spring, I learned that Twayne was interested in a critical biography on Zelazny; by that summer I had taken on the project. The book, as I conceive it, is meant as a resource and guide for those readers who are interested in knowing something of what shaped the man who writes the stories. A large amount of the text deals with backgrounds and sources and shows how Zelazny has incorporated his broad, eclectic education and experience into his fiction.

Zelazny's fiction and essays are used to illustrate information that I learned more informally through letters and conversations.

I supplemented the usual library research and the previously mentioned correspondence with various meetings with Zelazny. In November 1990, with the assistance of the Faculty Research and Development Fund at Lynchburg College, I went to Santa Fe and spent nearly a week working with Zelazny. We toured places where he had set portions of the latter Amber novels, visited museums he had used to research *Eye of Cat,* and talked for hours. That trip gave me an essay ("Zelazny's Santa Fe") and a greater sense of what forces unite the variety of Zelazny's interests.

Additional meetings were held at a variety of science fiction conventions. We met twice at Magnum Opus Convention in South Carolina, the first time in April 1991. The next year, Diana Bringardner invited me to come back as a guest, and Zelazny and I presented a panel on the in-process book. The thoughtful questions from the audience were extremely encouraging and helped to shape some of the issues that I chose to deal with in various chapters. My thanks to Diana.

Other conventions deserve my thanks for making possible my meeting with Zelazny without crossing the country. RoVaCon here in South Central Virginia brought Zelazny in as a guest in October 1991. Wolfcon in Starkville, Mississippi, invited me to join them in September 1992 to talk about the just-completed manuscript. Thank you, Glenn Simpson and crew.

Numerous people deserve acknowledgment for their contributions to this work. Lynchburg College contributed regular financial support to the research of the project. On a more personal level, my colleagues in the English Department, with their frequent and enthusiastic inquiries as to the progress of the book, encouraged me as I struggled to fit writing into my teaching schedule.

Kathy Curran deserves thanks, not just for starting me on this project, but for reading completed chapters and offering comments when I was too close to the book to be objective. Finally, my husband, David Davies, is due my thanks for his patience, interest, and support. Without his encouragement, the book could not have been completed.

Chronology

1937	Roger Zelazny born 13 May, Cleveland, Ohio.
1943-1949	Attends Noble School, Euclid, Ohio.
1949-1952	Attends Euclid Junior High School, Euclid, Ohio.
1952-1955	Attends Euclid Senior High School, Euclid, Ohio.
1954	Publishes a poem entitled "Diet" and two short stories, "Mr. Fuller's Revolt" and "The Darkness Is Harsh" in *Eucuyo*, the school's literary magazine. Later sells "Mr. Fuller's Revolt" to *Literary Cavalcade*.
1955	Publishes a poem entitled "Slush, Slush, Slush" and a short story, "Youth Eternal," in *Eucuyo*.
1955-1959	Attends Western Reserve University, Cleveland, Ohio. Majors in psychology, but changes major to English; graduates with B.A. in English.
1957	Wins Finley Foster Poetry Prize.
1958	Publishes a poem entitled "The Man without a Shadow" and a short story, "The Outward Sign," in *Skyline*, the university's literary magazine.
1959	Wins second Finley Foster Poetry Prize and the Holden Essay Award.
1959-1960	Attends Columbia University, New York, for graduate work in English. Specializes in Elizabethan and Jacobean drama.
1960	Joins Ohio National Guard. Writes master's thesis, "Two Traditions and Cyril Tourneur."
1962	Receives M.A. in English from Columbia. Publishes "Passion Play" in *Amazing* and "Horseman" in *Fantastic*. Begins work as claims representative for Social Security Administration in Cleveland.

1963   "A Rose for Ecclesiastes," for which Zelazny receives his
            first Hugo nomination, appears in *Fantasy and Science
            Fiction*. Publishes over a dozen other short stories in
            Amazing, Fantastic, and *New Worlds*.

1964   Publishes several more short stories, including "The
            Graveyard Heart" and "Lucifer." Is involved in a severe
            automobile accident in which he and his fiancée, Sharon
            Steberl, are injured. His father, Joseph Zelazny, dies
            suddenly on 25 November. Marries Sharon Steberl on 5
            December.

1965   "Devil Car" nominated for a Hugo. Also publishes sev-
            eral other stories including "The Doors of His Face, the
            Lamps of His Mouth" and "Passage to Dilfar" (the first
            story featuring recurring character Dilvish the Damned).
            Separates from Sharon Steberl in late summer.

1966   Wins Hugo for ". . . And Call Me Conrad." Wins Nebulas
            for "He Who Shapes" (novella) and "The Doors of His
            Face, the Lamps of His Mouth" (novelette). Publishes
            This Immortal and *The Dream Master*, novel expan-
            sions of ". . . And Call Me Conrad" and "He Who
            Shapes." Divorced from Sharon Steberl. Marries Judith
            Alene Callahan 20 August.

1967   Publishes *Isle of the Dead* and *Lord of Light* (novels),
            Four for Tomorrow (collection), and several shorter
            pieces.

1967-1968   Secretary-treasurer, Science Fiction Writers of America.

1968   Wins Hugo for *Lord of Light*. Edits *Nebula Award Sto-
            ries Three*. Publishes only five short stories.

1969   Publishes *Creatures of Light and Darkness* and *Damna-
            tion Alley*. Of the shorter pieces published, several are
            chapters from *Creatures of Light and Darkness*. Resigns
            from Social Security Administration to write full-time.

1970   Publishes *Nine Princes in Amber*.

1971   Publishes *Jack of Shadows* and *The Doors of His Face,
            the Lamps of His Mouth and Other Stories*. Son, Devin,
            born.

1972   Publishes *The Guns of Avalon*. Wins the Prix Apollo for the French edition of *Isle of the Dead*.

1973   Publishes *Today We Chose Faces* and *To Die in Italbar*.

1974   Publishes "The Engine at Heartspring's Center."

1975   Publishes *Sign of the Unicorn* and *Doorways in the Sand* in serial. Publishes *Sign of the Unicorn* in hardcover. Moves to Santa Fe, New Mexico.

1976   Wins both the Nebula and the Hugo for "Home is the Hangman" (novella). *Doorways in the Sand* selected as one of the Best Books for Young Adults by the American Library Association. Publishes *Doorways in the Sand*, *My Name is Legion*, *The Hand of Oberon*, *Bridge of Ashes*, and *Deus Irae* (in collaboration with Philip K. Dick). Son, Jonathan Trent, born.

1977   *The Courts of Chaos* published in serial. Movie version of *Damnation Alley* released.

1978   Publishes *The Courts of Chaos* and *The Illustrated Roger Zelazny* (in collaboration with Gray Morrow).

1979   Publishes *Roadmarks* and *The Chronicles of Amber* (collected novels in two volumes). Daughter, Shannon, born.

1980   Wins Balrog Award for "The Last Defender of Camelot." Publishes *Changeling*, *The Last Defender of Camelot* (collection), and *When Pussywillows Last in the Catyard Bloomed* (poetry).

1981   Publishes *Madwand*, *The Changing Land*, *A Rhapsody in Amber* (chapbook), and *To Spin is Miracle Cat* (poetry).

1982   Wins Hugo for "Unicorn Variation." Publishes *Eye of Cat*, *Dilvish, The Damned* (collection) and *Coils* (in collaboration with Fred Saberhagen).

1983   Publishes *Unicorn Variations* (collection).

1984   Wins Balrog Award for *Unicorn Variations*, wins Daicon Award for Japanese translation of the same collection.

1985   Publishes *Trumps of Doom*.

1986   Wins Hugo for "24 Views of Mount Fuji by Hokusai." Locus Award for "Best Fantasy Novel" for *Trumps of Doom*. Publishes *Blood of Amber*.

1987   Wins Hugo for "Permafrost." Publishes *Sign of Chaos* and *A Dark Travelling*. The latter is selected for the American Library Association's Booklist "Science Fiction Highlights for the Eighties."

1988   Publishes *Roger Zelazny's Visual Guide to Castle Amber* (with Neil Randall).

1989   Publishes *Knight of Shadows* and *Frost and Fire* (collection).

1990   Publishes *The Black Throne* (in collaboration with Fred Saberhagen) and *The Mask of Loki* (in collaboration with Thomas T. Thomas).

1991   Publishes *Prince of Chaos*, *Gone to Earth* (collection) *Bring Me the Head of Prince Charming* (in collaboration with Robert Sheckley).

1992   Publishes *Way Up High* and *Here There Be Dragons* (with art by Vaughan Bode), *Flare* (in collaboration with Thomas T. Thomas), and "Come Back to the Killing Ground, Alice, My Love" (novelette).

1993   Publishes *A Night in the Lonesome October* and *If At Faust You Don't Succeed* (in collaboration with Robert Sheckley).

Chapter One

Roger Zelazny

Formative Years

When Roger Zelazny was growing up in Euclid, Ohio, the area was largely rural. The house on East 250th Street in which he lived with his parents, Joseph and Josephine Sweet Zelazny, was set on an acre of land on a dirt road surrounded by fields and woods. Lake Erie was a few miles away, close enough to reach for a walk on the beaches.

Zelazny's heritage is primarily a mixture of Polish and Irish. His mother was American-born, his father was born in Europe:

> My father was born in Ripon, Poland – only there was no Poland then. It wasn't restored in this century until the WWI peace settlement. The last partitioning had divided it amongst Austria, Prussia & Tsarist Russia. My dad's part had belonged to the Tsar. The name comes from the word "zelazno" which means "iron," as the family included many blacksmiths down the years. . . . My mother's is the Irish side of the family, [with] a few other things tossed in on her paternal grandfather's side.[1]

Although his parents were from large families, each one of seven children, Roger Zelazny was an only child. He was thus solitary by circumstance and by nature. His closest friend in his early years was Carl Yoke. Zelazny describes the friendship as follows:

> I had one close friend, Carl Yoke, from Noble Elementary School through Shore Junior High and Euclid Senior High, and fortunately he remains my friend to this day. . . . He had two younger brothers, and he was brilliant and athletic. I really think we first became acquainted because of alphabetized classroom seating. Summers, we rode our bikes together during the day, took long walks at night discussing heavy existentialist stuff, teenage gossip, girls, books, life. I never knew I needed a friend till I met him.[2]

Today, Yoke is a college professor who among his credits lists several papers and the first biography on Zelazny and his works.

Ron Dobler, with whom Zelazny attended high school and college, is another person with whom a friendship has survived to the
present day. In college, when Zelazny captained the epee squad,
Dobler captained the saber squad. Dobler also encouraged Zelazny
to write poetry. Luke, the close friend of Merlin, protagonist of the
latter five Amber novels, owes his height, red hair, and good looks as
much to Ron Dobler as to his biological father, Brand.

Zelazny knew that he wanted to be a writer from a very early age
and set out writing and studying how stories were constructed by
the time he was 10 or 11 years old. His first typewriter was a gift from
his father when he was 11:

> My dad worked for the Addressograph-Multigraph Company, & when they
> switched from manual to electric machines they allowed employees to pur-
> chase the old uprights. He knew that I wanted to be a writer & asked me
> whether I wanted one. I said, "Yes," of course. I still have it, though I seldom
> use it these days. It's an old Royal & weighs about 30lb. Still works fine.
> (letter, 9 October 1989)

Zelazny taught himself to touch type and continued writing. He
recalls that soon after perfecting his typing, "I learned how to prepare manuscripts for professional submission. I sent out my first
story, an imitation Ray Bradbury Mars piece, to John W. Campbell,
who wasn't even buying Bradbury's stuff. Innocence" ("Aikido
Black," 4). Zelazny's efforts during this time also include a series of
stories written in collaboration with Yoke, entitled *The Record*, about
the mishaps of two monsters named Zlaz and Yok.

In his teens, Zelazny made his first concerted effort to sell his fiction. Except for the short story "Mr. Fuller's Revolt," published in
The Literary Cavalcade in 1954, his only publications were in school
literary magazines. After numerous rejections, he decided he needed
more experience to write fiction well. Rather than stopping writing
entirely, however, he shifted his focus to poetry.

College and Beyond

After high school, Zelazny attended Western Reserve University
(today part of Case Western Reserve) in Cleveland as a day student.
He began as a psychology major, but switched to English in his ju-

nior year when he began to consider how he was going to support himself after college: "I began wondering what I'd do after graduation to support the writing efforts. Get a grad degree or two and teach, I supposed. Then, looking at the mazes and breathing the air of the lab, I asked myself, 'Is it really Psych that you want to teach?' " ("Aikido Black," 14). One of Zelazny's habits while in college was to audit without credit any course that seemed interesting. This practice provided something of a structure for his accumulating knowledge and foreshadowed the reading program that he would develop for himself in later years.

Following graduation from Reserve, Zelazny left Ohio in 1959 to attend Columbia University in New York for graduate work in English. In a year, he completed his coursework for a master's degree with a concentration in the Elizabethan and Jacobean playwrights and continued his practice of auditing courses outside of his area. He also kept writing poetry. He completed his thesis, but his advisor did not pass it in time for him to graduate in the spring.

In 1960, since he could not take the comprehensive exams until his thesis was passed, he decided to enlist in the Ohio National Guard rather than waiting to be drafted. As a member of the 137th Artillery Battalion he underwent six months of active duty, first basic training at Fort Knox, Kentucky, then advanced individual training on missiles at Fort Bliss, Texas.

When his first three-year stint in the service ended in 1963, Zelazny re-enlisted, but changed services:

> I was able to go over to the Army Reserve because a guy I knew in a fancy unit had offered to get me into it (the 2370th Civil Affairs Group – Arts, Monuments & Archives – cf. THIS IMMORTAL – the group specializing in moving into conquered countries during the occupation, to preserve national treasures). Later on, this was disbanded & I was able to get transferred into the 2350th Public Information Group – press-release people – & I finally wound up in a Psychological Warfare outfit before finally getting an Honorable Discharge. (letter, 28 October 1989)

Although Zelazny's six years in the military were part-time, the atmosphere and odd bits of knowledge he picked up there would continually crop up in his fiction.

In 1961, after finishing his active duty, Zelazny filed for unemployment and started writing again while hunting (without too much eagerness) for a job. "A Rose for Ecclesiastes," for which he would receive his first Hugo nomination in 1963, was written at this time. He also reviewed and resubmitted his thesis, which this time was not only accepted but also awarded honors. In February 1962, he took a job with the Social Security Administration as a claims representative. With a steady job, he now had to marshall his writing into an increasingly tight schedule:

> I went to Dayton & began training for a claims representative position [with] the Social Security Administration, & began writing stories in the evenings the same week I arrived there. I sold my 1st one on March 28, & 16 more that year. I passed my comps in May & [received] the degree. I applied for teaching jobs all over Ohio then, but things were tight & no offers came in, so I stayed with the [government] & kept writing, evenings. (letter, 28 October 1989)

Zelazny's job with Social Security would last until 1969, when he resigned to write full-time. Even while he was working in this most nonliterary of jobs, he found ways to use the experience to build his resources for writing: "I looked at people's hands and the gestures they made with them. I studied their faces, wondered about their clothing, their jewelry, their scars. I listened to them lie and tell what they thought was the truth."[3] He also became the resident expert in Chinese marriage customs.

Incidentally, the nameless protagonist of the stories collected in *I Am Legion* owes his evolution to a conversation about centralized identity records that Zelazny had with Bill Spangler, with whom he worked at the Social Security office in Baltimore.[4] In Lewis Briggs, the harried civil servant in *Isle of the Dead*, Zelazny parodies the convoluted rules and regulations of government bureaucracy.

During 1963, Zelazny also held a part-time job as a teacher at Fenn College, now Cleveland State, as an instructor of freshman English. He found that teaching took too much time and energy from his writing when added to his full-time job. He quit after one semester, passing the job on to his friend, Ron Dobler, who at that time was a high school teacher; now, like Carl Yoke, he has become a college English professor.

The year 1964 was a particularly difficult one for Zelazny. In the autumn, he and his fiancée, Sharon Steberl, were in an automobile accident outside of Mansfield, Ohio. Although Zelazny was not too severely injured, Steberl was injured seriously enough to delay their

October wedding. Thomas Monteleone, in his 1973 master's thesis dealing with some of Zelazny's works, identifies this car accident in 1964 as the source of the accident in Zelazny's novel *The Dream Master*, which kills the protagonist's wife and daughter. He also indicates that there may be some relationship between it and the general distrust of cars that shows up in Zelazny's fiction (Sanders, xxvi).

On 25 November Zelazny's father died unexpectedly. Although still adjusting to this shock, Zelazny went ahead with plans for his wedding and was married 5 December. The marriage did not work out, and he separated from his wife in late summer 1965; they were divorced in 1966.

Following his separation from Sharon Steberl, Zelazny accepted a promotion to claims policy specialist and relocated to Baltimore. Once settled, he continued to write each evening. His stories were now regularly nominated for various awards, and in 1966 he won his first Hugo for ". . . And Call Me Conrad" and his first Nebulas for "He Who Shapes" in the novella category and for "The Doors of His Face, the Lamps of His Mouth" in the novelette category. Later that same year he published his first two novels, *This Immortal* and *The Dream Master*. Both were expanded versions of his award-winning shorter works; ". . . And Call Me Conrad" had been shortened for magazine publication and Zelazny expanded "He Who Shapes" at the suggestion of author and editor Damon Knight. The year 1966 was also marked by a positive event unrelated to his writing, when on 20 August he married Judith Alene Callahan, with whom he had worked at the Social Security Administration.

The mid-1960s were a time of both high productivity and high visibility for Zelazny. Award nominations were so frequent that his own pieces competed against one another for the Hugo Award in the novelette category in both 1966 ("This Moment of the Storm" and "For a Breath I Tarry") and 1967 ("This Mortal Mountain" and "The Keys to December"). In 1968 his novel *Lord of Light* won the Hugo.

An effect of coming into prominence in the mid-1960s was that Zelazny was grouped with Harlan Ellison, Samuel R. Delany, Thomas Disch, and Norman Spinrad, among others, as an American "New Wave" writer. The term was coined by editor Judith Merril and quickly adopted by others:

> We were lumped together, despite our differences, because we were similar in representing a reaction to the sf [science fiction] of the 40s & 50s which, while containing some fine ideas & colorful stories, was not particularly noted for the quality of the writing. . . . A [number] of us simultaneously began importing stuff that was old hat in general fiction but new to sf, at about the same time – stream of consciousness, impressionism, stylistic flourishes, a greater emphasis on characterization. . . . Most of us deny there was such a thing as a New Wave "movement" because there was no overall plan or manifesto, many of us were not even acquainted in those days, & we are all sufficiently individualistic to dislike being categorized. (letter, 4 February 1990)

One "New Wave" writer with whom Zelazny was acquainted was Harlan Ellison, but their initial meeting had more to do with their both having grown up in Ohio than their writing. Their first meeting was in 1955 at the World Science Fiction Convention in Cleveland, Ohio. Introduced by Gail Gianasi, a mutual acquaintance, as "two people who are going to be famous sf writers one day" (letter, 4 February 1990), they did not meet again until 11 years later, when both received Hugo Awards at the 1966 World Science Fiction Convention, again in Cleveland. Their friendship has continued over the years, extending professionally to collaboration on one short story, "Come to Me Not in Winter's White," and Zelazny's contribution to Ellison's *Dangerous Visions* collections.

Another of the New Wave writers with whom Zelazny developed a friendship was Samuel R. Delany. In his article "Faust and Archimedes," Delany recalls his encounter with one of Zelazny's stories:

> A few months before I first went to Europe, a young woman music student came knocking on my door, waving a copy of *The Magazine of Fantasy and Science Fiction* with an absolutely obsessed expression: "Have you read this, Chip? Have you *read* this? Who is he? Do you know anything about him? What has he written before?"
>
> *The Doors of His Face, the Lamps of His Mouth* was headed by one of F&SF's less informative blurbs. I read it; that copy of the magazine went with me to Europe. I gave it to half a dozen people to read.[5]

Zelazny and Delany did eventually meet and become friends. Zelazny credits Delany with finding a sympathetic editor to publish his experimental novel *Creatures of Light and Darkness*; the dedication of the novel, "To Chip Delany, Just Because" acknowledges his debt.[6] Delany's novella *We in Some Strange Power's Employ, Move on a Rigorous Line* contains a character who introduces himself as follows: " 'My name's Roger . . . ' followed by something Polish and unpronounceable that began with a Z and ended in Y."[7] Knowing that a connection might be made between this character (a rather unsavory person) and Zelazny, Delany phoned Zelazny. Zelazny recalls that Delany read him sections from the just completed work "to see whether I was in any way offended. I assured him it was just the opposite" (letter, 7 April 1990).

The recognition and praise Zelazny received also had its negative corollary. Especially as Zelazny moved away from the shorter pieces on which his reputation had rested and into novel-length works, he began to come under critical attack. A piece that is representative of the general tone in reviews and articles is Richard Cowper's "a rose is a rose is a rose . . . in search of roger zelazny," published in 1977. Cowper recounts his initial enchantment and then eventual disenchantment with Zelazny's work. "Barely out of his diapers," he begins, "Zelazny had been hailed as a genius; at one bound he had seemingly scaled the ultimate summit and boldly planted his flag upon it."[8] He goes on to compare Zelazny with the youthful Lord Byron, who found himself famous too quickly. After briefly analyzing a number of Zelazny's novels and noting his lack of "creative discipline" and inability to control his style and characterization, Cowper concludes that Zelazny had failed the test of a major writer and, despite his talent and energy, had not yet written a major work.

Cowper's essay, while highly personal, does reflect a vocal portion of the reaction to Zelazny's writing following his initial, enthusiastic reception. For his 1980 annotated bibliography of Zelazny's works, Joseph Sanders read the majority of the available letters, reviews, and criticism and then analyzed the bulk of it as follows:

> Much of this attention has been favorable, and even the negative criticism has expressed a high regard for Zelazny's ability. Some critics, however, have voiced irritation when Zelazny has not done exactly *what they expected*, even though they may have misinterpreted his work. The two most serious misinterpretations, which show up repeatedly in the critical studies . . . concern Zelazny's use of myth and his prose style. (xv)

Sanders goes on to discuss in great detail both Zelazny's use of myth and the development of his prose style, arguing – in a vein similar to his 1978 article "Zelazny: Unfinished Business"[9] – that Zelazny's writing is a result of his "willingness to forego the safe and pre-dictable effects that would have kept readers comfortable" (xxiv).

Once Zelazny resigned from the Social Security Administration in 1969 to write full-time, a trend in his work habits away from shorter fiction to novel-length fiction became confirmed. In the introduction to his collection *The Last Defender of Camelot*, Zelazny explains the reason for the shift:

> I had started out as a short story writer, and I still enjoy writing short stories though I no longer do nearly as many as I used to in a year's time. The reason is mainly economic. I went full-time in the late 60's, and it is a fact of writing life that, word for word, novels work harder for their creators when it comes to providing for the necessities and joys of existence. Which would sound cold and cynical, except that I enjoy writing novels, too.[10]

Zelazny's artistic preference, however, remains for shorter works:

> Preference . . . ? Short stories (by which I mean to include novelettes & novellas). You say everything that you want to say & then you stop, [with] no concern over the length. No wasted motion. . . . It's a very pure form com-pared to the novel, & I love it; but nobody can make a living just doing shorts. (letter, 27 March 1990)

Interestingly, even after the bulk of his energy went into novels, the majority of his recent awards have continued to be in the shorter fiction categories. "Unicorn Variation" and "Permafrost" won Hugos in 1982 and 1987 in the novelette category; "24 Views of Mount Fuji by Hokusai" won a Hugo in the novella category in 1986. Zelazny's transition into writing full-time was not easy or painless. His publica-tion chronology suggests that he simply began producing a novel or more a year fairly effortlessly. The facts are somewhat different.

Full-Time Writer

Zelazny's first novel following his resignation from the Social Security Administration in 1969 was *Nine Princes in Amber*, the first of the highly popular Amber books, which, as of this writing, have become a 10-book series. Although *Nine Princes* was published at this time, it had actually been written around 1967; its sequel, *The Guns of*

Avalon, which was published in 1972, had been shelved unfinished in 1969. Newer works were written with a greater awareness of the pressure to produce for a market. Zelazny wrote *To Die in Italbar*, published in 1973, aware that he no longer had a paycheck to fall back on. This pressure led to what he views as his weakest book:

> I wrote it in the month after I quit work for the [government] to write full-time. I felt the pressure to produce that first year & I dashed that one off extremely quickly, for the money. It took me about a year to achieve a sense of balance in these matters (if I ever actually achieved it). (letter, 17 August 1989)

Despite this apprehension, Zelazny continued to experiment with form, structure, and language, applying some of the techniques that he had used for shorter fiction to longer works. Both the novels *Today We Choose Faces* and *Doorways in the Sand* are evidence of his continuing desire to develop his abilities as a writer even at this time. *Today We Choose Faces* was published in a form that did not reflect Zelazny's original, more innovative structure for the novel:

> It was not published the way I wrote it. That which is Part II in the book was really my opening section. That which is Part I was really Part II, the flashback which becomes revealed when that particular pin is pulled. My editor claimed I was asking too much of the reader with my original structure. I was younger & more in need of the money at the time & couldn't afford to argue [with] him about it. I still prefer it the way I wrote it. (letter, 11 February 1989)

Doorways in the Sand also evolved around an experiment in structure. Zelazny notes:

> Once I knew what the story was to be, I ran it, a piece at a time, through a flashback machine, using the suspense-heightening flashback trick so frequently and predictably that the practice intentionally parodied the device itself.[11]

Another way in which *Doorways in the Sand* is experimental is that it was Zelazny's first attempt at an extended humorous piece. His active sense of humor had always made itself evident through the puns and word play that riddle even his most serious works, but he had never tried an entirely humorous novel. Perhaps the fact that he achieves this goal is the reason the novel is often classified as young adult fiction when Zelazny wrote it for adults.

While Zelazny's professional life settled more securely around his writing, his private life was becoming more family oriented. In 1971, his son, Devin, was born. In 1975, Zelazny felt comfortable enough with his ability to support himself and his family to consider leaving Baltimore. After a visit to friends in the area, Zelazny relocated to Santa Fe, New Mexico. Santa Fe provided the mixture of rural and urban qualities that Zelazny was seeking. Zelazny explains:

> [T]he town met almost all our needs. We were tired of large urban centers, but we wanted the amenities – such as good restaurants, bookstores, theater. The climate, the picturesque quality and the proximity of wilderness and skiing helped. The tricultural mixture made the place very interesting. The absence of heavy industry was pleasing. It felt like a good place to write and raise kids.[12]

Zelazny still lives in a "substantially augmented" version of house he and Judy purchased in 1975, which is set on an acre lot bordering the Pecos Wilderness. In 1976 Zelazny's second son, Jonathan Trent, usually called Trent, was born, and in 1979, his daughter, Shannon. In the late 1970s Zelazny's mother moved from Ohio into her own home in Santa Fe, thus bringing all his immediate family into easy reach.

The mid-1970s were a busy time for Zelazny professionally as well as personally. Between 1975 and 1982 rarely a year passed without at least one novel being published. Several ancillary works were published as well. In 1976 alone he published five novel-length works, including *Deus Irae*, written in collaboration with Philip K. Dick, and *My Name Is Legion*, a collection of three stories featuring his nameless protagonist. The collection includes the Hugo- and Nebula-winning novella "Home Is the Hangman." During this time he also expanded the Amber series to five books and wrote two of his more structurally innovative books, *Roadmarks* and *Eye of Cat*. In 1977 his novel *Damnation Alley* was made into a movie that bears little resemblance to Zelazny's original work.

Between 1983 and 1990 his writing pace slowed quite a bit as he focused his energies on the reading program he had designed for himself some years before. In 1984 his only publications were three short works – all solicited for theme collections. In 1985 he restarted the Amber series, which had been dormant since the publication of *The Courts of Chaos* in 1978, shocking some of the series' fans by switching narrators from Corwin to his son, Merlin. In 1987, he became one of the founding writers for George R. R. Martin's Wild Cards shared worlds series, contributing to the first two collections, *Wild Cards* and *Aces High*, and the "mosaic novel" *Down and Dirty*.[13]

But lest Zelazny's writings in the mid- to late 1980s be quickly dismissed as comparatively light, it must be noted that during this time he also published "24 Views of Mount Fuji by Hokusai" and "Permafrost," both of which won Hugo awards.

Another shift in Zelazny's writing habits during this time was the increasing emphasis on collaboration with other writers. He had previously collaborated with Philip K. Dick on *Deus Irae* and with Fred Saberhagen on *Coils*, but during the late 1980s he took on several more collaborative projects. Two of these were published in 1990, *The Black Throne*, again with Fred Saberhagen, and *The Mask of Loki*, with Thomas T. Thomas. A third, *Bring Me the Head of Prince Charming* with Robert Sheckley, was published in 1991. A second collaborative effort with Thomas, *Flare*, was published in 1992. Further collaborations with Sheckley include *If at Faust You Don't Succeed*, published in 1993, and a proposed novel set mainly in the sixteenth century and tentatively titled *Imitations of Immortality, or Venice Preserve*.

The early 1990s show Zelazny moving away from the more contemplative habits of the previous decade. "Come Back to the Killing Ground, Alice, My Love," his most recent novelette, appeared in the August 1992 issue of *Amazing Stories*. The novel *A Night in the Lonesome October* was released in August 1993. Another Wild Cards story, "The Long Sleep," appears in volume 13, *Card Sharks*. He has also begun work on a three-book series tentatively titled *Donnerjack, of Virtu*, *The Gods of Virtu*, and *Virtu, Virtu*. This "parable for the machine age" is to consist of his longest novels since *Lord of Light*. Another on-going project is a non-science fiction novel with Gerald Hausman entitled *Wilderness*.

Chapter Two

What Shaped Zelazny: Literary and Educational Influences

Formal Education

For many authors, a general survey of formal education and perhaps a notation of research techniques and a few influential books are adequate to document their intellectual development. Zelazny, however, in education as in so many other areas, breaks the established pattern. While his formal education through his master's degree was instrumental in shaping the writer he has become, the greater part of his education began after his formal training was completed. To attempt to comprehend Zelazny as a writer, one must understand the development of his education from the formal through the informal.

Carl Yoke, a schoolmate of Zelazny's from first grade through high school, assesses the young Zelazny as a "bright but undisciplined student."[1] Conversation with Zelazny confirms that while he enjoyed learning, he was not overly fond of classroom studies. In fact, many of his reminiscences about things learned at that time begin with readings discovered during a study hall or free period. Therefore, the influence of three particularly important instructors from high school cannot be overlooked, especially considering that Zelazny went on to college and then to graduate school at a time when neither was the routine career choice that it since has become.

One very influential teacher was Ruby Olsen. Although she never taught Zelazny in the classroom, Olsen formed a small creative writing club and encouraged the somewhat reclusive Zelazny to join. The club itself was not a formal workshop but an informal forum for discussion of both readings and ideas. Sometimes students would bring in their writings to be critiqued by the other members. To encourage students to write, Olsen would share her own poetry. Perhaps the greatest indicator of both the club and Olsen as influences on Zelazny is that today he still recalls the names of the five students (which included Carl Yoke) in the club.

Zelazny met Myron Gordon in a more conventional classroom setting when he decided that a class in journalism was a logical complement to his already confirmed interest in writing. Gordon encouraged Zelazny to become features editor for the school newspaper. Zelazny recalls Gordon as a young man, still working on his master's degree, who would often come in and talk while Zelazny was in the paper's office. Being features editor fed Zelazny's desire to see his own work in print. It also showed him the value of developing some personal discipline to meet deadlines.

Another highly influential teacher was Harold Blackburn, one of Zelazny's English teachers. Zelazny recalls how Blackburn's comments shaped the texts he was reading outside the classroom:

> He once said something in class about Hemingway's OLD MAN AND THE SEA, & that afternoon I got excused from study hall & went to spend the period in the school library . . . I discovered I'd already read all the magazines I liked & there was no new sf in, so I recalled Blackburn's comments, turned up a copy of OLD MAN . . . and began reading it. (letter, 13 March 1990)

Learning that Zelazny was taking his suggestions seriously and that he wanted to be a writer, Blackburn continued to make suggestions, including one that had considerable influence on the development of Zelazny's style:

> At one point, he said, "There are three things you must read – [Tolstoy's] WAR AND PEACE, Joyce's ULYSSES, and [Proust's] REMEMBRANCE OF THINGS PAST – for a very special reason." His reason was interesting. He said that once you read them you realized that among them they covered the entire spectrum of human experience – war, peace, mysticism, rationality, class structures, every sort of social problem, every sort of character; & that they also contain all of the literary devices and approaches: the comic, the tragic, the Classic, the Romantic, realism, naturalism, the introspective as well as the external approaches to characterization, experimentalism . . . et cetera. Read them, he told me, & you'll have touchstones for anything you read afterwards. . . . I guess he did instill a reflex, as I find myself on occasion comparing new things to them, only half-realizing what I'm doing. (letter, 14 March 1990)

A fine example of how Blackburn's suggestion shaped Zelazny's later prose can be found in *Blood of Amber*. Zelazny notes that at one point he deliberately styled his prose after a sentence from Proust's *Within a Budding Grove*, "which I thought delicate & delightful & also felt to state the whole theme of the lost past recaptured" (letter, 21 March 1989). A comparison of the passages shows Zelazny's stylistic debt. Proust's selection reads:

> And as the average span of life, the relative longevity of our memories of poetical sensations is much greater than that of our memories of what the heart has suffered, long after the sorrows that I once felt on Gilberte's account have faded and vanished, there has survived them the pleasure that I still derive – whenever I close my eyes and read, as it were upon the face of a sundial, the minutes that are recorded between a quarter past twelve and one o'clock in the month of May – from seeing myself once again strolling and talking thus with Madame Swann beneath her parasol, as though in the colored shade of a wisteria bower.[2]

The passage from *Blood of Amber* that Zelazny modeled on Proust reads:

> Memories of sorrow, betrayal, suffering are strong but they do fade, whereas interludes such as this, when I close my eyes and regard the calendar of my days, somehow outlast them, as I see myself riding with Vinta Bayle under morning skies where the houses and fences are stone and stray seabirds call, there in the wine country to the east of Amber, and the scythe of Time has no power in this corner of the heart.[3]

The influence of these three teachers became part of the background that Zelazny took with him to Western Reserve University. Here, as in high school, his study habits were less than conventional. Starting as a psychology major, he switched to English when the department's clinical psychology emphasis shifted to a more behaviorist approach. He was also beginning to consider teaching English as a complementary career to writing and knew that he would need to go on for advanced degree work in that area.

College permitted Zelazny to structure his own class choices more freely than in high school, and he took full advantage of this freedom. One of the habits he developed in college was that of auditing courses that did not fit his formal schedule. He describes the process as follows:

I'd attend the first class & sit in the back. I'd discover quickly then whether
the lecturer was an attendance-taker. . . . Then I'd see how I liked the introductory lecture. If I did, I'd go and buy the books, do the reading, attend the
lectures & take notes – everything but exams and papers. (letter, 9 October
1989)

In this way, Zelazny was able to multiply the opportunities available
to him in college. Among the courses he audited was one called
"Magic, the Devil, and Witchcraft," through which he developed his
admiration for Sir James Frazer, whose *Golden Bough* helped to provide a framework for the mythology that he had been reading independently up to that point.

Although still interested in writing professionally, Zelazny went
on to Columbia's graduate school to earn his M.A. in English. At this
point, he had not decided whether he would focus on writing poetry
or prose. He did think that a background in literature would be useful no matter what his focus and that teaching would be a good profession to follow while writing. At Columbia he took a variety of
courses and continued his practice of auditing any course that interested him but did not fit his curriculum. In this fashion, he sometimes put in as much as 40 lecture hours a week.

For his thesis, he chose to write on Elizabethan drama. "Two
Traditions and Cyril Tourneur: An Examination of Morality and
Humor Comedy Conventions in 'The Revenger's Tragedy' " is a quite
readable piece that demonstrates Zelazny's long-time interest in
intermingling serious and comic themes. Zelazny's choice of a thesis
area is also evidence of his abiding enthusiasm for drama.

To this point, Zelazny has not written a play; the closest he has
come is the first outline for Twentieth Century Fox's "Dreamscape"
and the "closet drama" in *Creatures of Light and Darkness*. He attends the theater regularly, and in an outburst of enthusiasm once
commented: "I love the theater so much that I could see a fresh play
every night for a year and not get tired of watching them" (letter, 12
November 1989). His interest in drama goes beyond that of spectator
and literary critic to shape his prose style extensively. Two books
that he notes as influences are *The Idea of a Theater* and *The
Human Image in Dramatic Literature*, both by Francis Fergusson:

I recall some small feeling of enlightenment on his discussion of Stanislavsky-
Boleslavsky theory [with] the reducing of the entire action of a play to a single

statement consisting of the infinitive form of a transitive verb & its object, & letting everything in the play contribute to its realization. (letter, 12 April 1989)

Another influential book, not only for its approach to drama but to the craft of writing in general, was Lajos Egri's *The Art of Dramatic Writing: Its Basis in the Creative Interpretation of Human Motives*.

Informal Reading Program

Although Zelazny's formal education ended when he received his master's degree in English from Columbia in 1962, he has continued acquiring information through a curriculum that he designed in 1971 and continues to follow – with some adaptations – to this day. Early in his career Zelazny was aware that his writing style was responsible for a large part of the attention that he was getting:

> Somewhere in *Remembrance of Things Past*, Proust talks about a writer (I forget the name he gives him) & indicates that he was once a young, flashy author who outlasted those days & whose literary devices were by then old hat, but that it did not matter because he kept going "on the strength of intellect." For some reason, this impressed me very much & I thought of it often, back in the 60s and 70s. I knew when I was playing word-games & writing stream of consciousness & throwing in extra doses of metaphor that if that sort of thing were to catch on in sf there would come a time when it was common property & a lot of other people could or would be doing the same thing. So, recalling Proust's character, I decided that while stylistic eccentricities were good for getting attention initially I had better decide on the proper pattern to pursue & continue my education within it. (letter, 19 May 1989)

Zelazny's reading program did not formalize instantly, but evolved as he began to fill in what he perceived as limitations that might one day restrict his development as a writer. One of the earliest parts of his program involved building up a "mental picture of the world, topographically & culturally" (letter, 9 June 1989). This portion of his program was put to an immediate test when he wrote his first novel *This Immortal*, large parts of which were set in Greece, a country he had never visited:

> For a section of THIS IMMORTAL, I recall picking up a street guide of Athens (in a Fodor's travel guide), imagining the city as having been bombed since

the present & restored, & then walking Conrad through it, drawing upon resonances from the stuff that was already in place. Fooled John Brunner, a frequent visitor to Greece, into thinking I knew the area well. Fooled Samuel
Delany, too. (letter, 9 June 1989)

Another area in which Zelazny read extensively was nature writing and ecology. This interest had its roots in an informal appreciation of nature that began in his Ohio childhood:

We had an acre abutting large undeveloped areas of fields & woods in which I
used to walk a lot as a kid. The more I got interested in trees, insects & animals the more I felt the seasons & the daily weather scene as a part of everything else & the more I paid attention to it. (letter, 7 April 1990)

While still young, he discovered the writings of the naturalist Ernest
Thompson Seton. Seton became the first of the nature writers
Zelazny would absorb. A list of favorite authors in the area includes
Edwin Way Teale, Sigurd F. Olsen, Anne LaBastille, Aldo Leopold,
John Terres, Joseph Wood Krutch, and Robert Finch. Zelazny com-
ments on his interest:

There is a lot of good writing in the area, though in many ways it is an odd
category. I sort of had to stumble into it as a genre, but found that the better
writers in it repaid attention by combining many of my interests in the humanities as well as the sciences. I'd often felt it would have been interesting to
have taken a course in it, beginning with, say, WALDEN, running through
John Muir & John Burroughs & maybe Ernest Thompson Seton, down
through the more recent ones. (letter, 15 August 1989)

Certainly, the effect of Zelazny's reading in this area is immediately
evident in his fiction, in the details of worldscaping in *Isle of the
Dead*, for example, or of accelerated evolution in "The Keys to
December."

Despite the unifying elements offered by genres like nature
writing, as Zelazny continued to broaden his educational background he began to feel that his program lacked a major organizing
principle and began to cast about for a congenial structure:

I selected da Vinci's mind for a model, studying his life & works for some time.
While his drawbacks obviously lay in the scattering of his forces, I saw there
the virtue of doing something other than merely educating my own interests;

& I began to feel that anything could be interesting if one approached it properly. This is what led me to aim for something of universality rather than specializing in certain subjects & writing mainly about them. (letter, 19 May 1989)

Zelazny's choice of da Vinci had an unanticipated result on his reading program when da Vinci's fascination with the human body lead Zelazny to investigate medicine:

I might have skimped on medicine had it not been for the [da Vinci] model, which made me take it on as a lifetime area of concern. It became a coming-together place at one corner of my consciousness; & the nature/ecology material occupies another. And both are where they are because of that Renaissance artist who saw life as a spectrum rather than a series of boxes. (letter, 28 September 1989)

Da Vinci, however, was an inadequate model on his own. Concerned that da Vinci's broad, eclectic interests might prove to be their own trap, Zelazny set out to find a theorist who could provide a balance to the da Vinci model. He found what he sought in the writings of Jacques Barzun:

When I considered da Vinci I was taken by the notion of building up a complete working model of the universe in one's mind, which seemed an overpowering task – as well as a disastrous one for [da Vinci] himself, tending to give him too many irons in the fire. A concept from Jacques Barzun's writings came to my aid about then, however; *viz.*, a sufficient accumulation of knowledge will grow. I don't mean by one's studiously, conscientiously adding to it either.

I believe that there is something like a "critical mass" in every area of learning, & that if one considers the information in that area till one achieves that point it becomes a part of the architecture of the mind rather than a mere assemblage of facts. (letter, 13 June 1989)

Zelazny set out to apply this theory in various areas of the sciences and humanities. He started by reading one book in each area of the sciences, preferring those with historical approaches to discover how the ideas developed. Then he began to read other books, aiming for a minimum of 10 books in each area. He also developed a "purely subjective" concept to guide this process: "the 'key book' – that is, the best book in the area for a particular person, after which anything else one reads becomes much clearer and more interesting" (letter, 13 June 1989).

In addition to educational theories, Zelazny took ideas for certain reading areas from Barzun. Barzun, himself a history professor, felt that a regular reading course in history was essential. Following Barzun's recommendation, Zelazny set out to read a general world history, choosing Will and Ariel Durant's 11-volume series for reasons of availability:

> I'd read a volume, slowly, then go off & read some other history books – any period that struck my fancy – for a break, before going on to read the next big volume. It took years that way, but when I finished the series I'd also read something like 60 other books in supplement. And I never quit after that. I liked it so well that I always have a History book going, & as soon as I finish it I start another. (letter, 27 June 1989)

Another area in which Zelazny began systematic reading because of Barzun was biography:

> He also recommended . . . biographies & autobiographies as a way of personalizing history. This was not exactly my favorite genre at the time but I decided to give it a try – all periods, all countries, all walks of life, from St. Augustine to the Marquis de Sade, from Shaka Zulu to Sir Laurence Olivier. He was right, of course. Now I start a new one as soon as I finish the current one here, too, & they fascinate me, like a series of low-budget reincarnations. (letter, 27 June 1989)

To his Barzun/da Vinci program, which tended to concentrate on nonfiction, Zelazny added a liberal dose of literature, both fiction and poetry. His early interest in becoming a poet had given him an acute interest in poetry, but he did not begin systematically reading it until quite a bit later:

> I added poetry, so as to read some every day, not solely for enjoyment, but because I felt it had beneficial effects on my prose. I didn't install it, though, at first . . . I think that it was about 1973 that I decided that I should read it regularly & began picking up volumes at the Johns Hopkins bookstore on my weekly visits there. They had a good poetry section. (letter, 19 October 1991)

Equally, he already read a large amount of fiction, but as demands on his time became more pressing, he developed a system for assuring that fiction would not be slighted. Although his fiction reading is not restricted to science fiction and fantasy, for professional reasons as well as personal preferences he reads a fair amount in the area:

> As to sf itself, I have mentioned that there were several periods when I didn't read much of it – most notably in the late 60s & early 70s. I just read enough to keep up [with] the area. It was around 1972, I believe, when a [number] of conversations with Tom Monteleone showed me that I might be falling behind on what was being done, that I resolved always to have a sf book going . . . I still try to mix in older classics that I'd missed along [with] the current stuff I want to keep up on. (letter, 19 October 1991)

This detailed reading program, added to his formal education, makes Zelazny one of the most versatile science fiction writers today. A closer look at how the material from the reading program detailed in the previous pages was directly incorporated into several novels provides a fascinating demonstration of how Zelazny's early resolve not to simply rest on a flashy style has been put into practice. Two of the novels best suited for this examination are *Bridge of Ashes* and *Roadmarks*, since these books are rooted in the historical and cultural tradition Zelazny has so assiduously sought to acquire.

Bridge of Ashes is one of Zelazny's self-admittedly "experimental" novels, in which he plays with the story-telling process. It is at times a difficult novel to read. Part of the difficulty comes from the structure. Part 1 begins with a series of short vignettes, each focused on the last minutes of the central figure's life. First, there is a primitive hunter, then an unidentified "man by the seaside" (6), who is easily recognizable as Archimedes. The next identifies himself as Flavius Claudius Julianus, the Roman emperor more commonly known as Julian. Julian is followed by da Vinci, da Vinci by Rousseau. After a brief return to a woman lamenting over the dying hunter, the scene shifts to the Marquis de Condorcet. Condorcet is followed by Gilbert Van Duyn, a fictional character, who is preparing to speak before the United Nations about a plan to prevent further pollution of the Earth. The section ends with a brief explanation by a mysterious "dark man" to Van Duyn that human history has been shaped by aliens who have manipulated humanity into an elaborate terraforming device, designed to create a world in which the aliens can thrive. Until the end of part 1, the reader really has no idea what is going on. Zelazny himself noted in his 1989 foreword to the novel that he had "some misgiving after the book had grown cool for me, wondering at the appropriateness of puzzling the reader for eighteen pages before beginning to show what was actually happening" (2).

The difficulties grow not only from the novel's structure but also from the central character, Dennis Guise. Dennis is a telepath of phenomenal powers. Whereas most telepaths in *Bridge of Ashes* can make contact only with minds within a 20-mile radius, even as an infant Dennis is able to make contact with minds much farther away. The trauma of being bombarded by too many thoughts at a young age sends Dennis into catatonic withdrawal. The therapy he begins at age 13 with telepathic therapist Lydia Dimanche appears to help only somewhat; even when Dennis does begin to emerge from catatonia, he has no personality of his own. Instead he fastens onto a few of the minds around him and adopts their actions, living their lives long distance.

Eventually, Dennis's parents move him to a hospital on the Moon, and in the isolation there he reveals a new telepathic strength, the ability to reach back through time and fasten on other minds, effectively becoming people who are long dead. Within these adopted personalities, Dennis begins to interact more and more with the people around him, but his own personality is still effectively under construction. Only when the last of these borrowed personalities becomes dormant does Dennis Guise emerge.

Dennis's choice of minds to fasten on is not governed by chance, but is eventually revealed to be the work of Lydia Dimanche, who is not only a telepathic therapist but also, it turns out, the same woman who mourned the dying hunter/god-king in part 1. As such, she has her own agenda, one that she shares with the hunter, the dark man of part 1. When Dennis realizes that Lydia has been directing the pattern of his recovery, he says to her: "I suddenly look upon you as the architect of my existence" (131). This realization reveals an interesting corollary to Zelazny's own theories regarding the effects of self-education:

> When I came to the conclusion years ago that everyone was like a carpenter who'd been given tools & supplies & then told to build something under siege conditions, I realized that, in the main, we create ourselves; & I wanted a mind that could be a weapon as well as a thing of knowledge and creation. I read educational theory while I was in Psychology; I even had a part-time job

in the Psych Dept's lab for 1 1/2 - 2 years. But one day I said, The hell with all the theories, take an engineering approach, find a highly successful working model & try to figure out how it got that way. After some deliberation involving Greek philosophers & Voltaire & Goethe, I settled on da Vinci as the specimen to place under study. (letter, 28 September 1989)

In fact, when one traces the various options that Zelazny considered and then discarded for his own educational model and compares them with the various minds that Dennis Guise adopts, there are some interesting parallels.

In the passage quoted above, Zelazny mentions that among the models he considered when designing his own program were "Greek philosophers & Voltaire & Goethe" before he settled on da Vinci. Interestingly, Dennis Guise begins his adoption of past memories with the Greek philosopher Archimedes. As Archimedes, he becomes absorbed in geometry, drawing figures "with near-mechanical perfection" (89). Dennis's next adopted personality is that of the Marquis de Condorcet, a social philosopher who lived at the time of the French Revolution. The events of Condorcet's life, including his *Sketch for a Historical Picture of the Progress of the Human Mind*, make him a more suitable model for Dennis than Voltaire would have been. But Voltaire is given a cameo through the scattered thoughts of his contemporary Rousseau in part 1 of the novel.

After Condorcet, Dennis adopts the personality and memories of Zelazny's own model, Leonardo da Vinci. While *Bridge of Ashes* devotes only three pages to each of the earlier incarnations, the da Vinci stage is given over twice as much. Da Vinci is also the only one of the personas to learn that he is in effect a parasite within another person. Whereas each of the other personas departs after enacting their death – Archimedes reacting as if to a sword cut, Condorcet by hanging himself, an act that nearly kills Dennis as well – da Vinci apparently departs of his own volition, troubled by the idea that he may be keeping someone else from emerging to full awareness. After the departure of da Vinci, Dennis finally comes into himself. As the novel progresses to its climactic confrontation with the aliens who have been manipulating the course of human history as a vast terraforming project, one realizes that Dennis embodies far more than the few people whose lives he has enacted. At this point, the short, first-person narratives from part 1 fall into place and Dennis comes into his own as the switchboard or contact point, whose phenomenal telepathic powers enable him to connect all of past humanity across time's "bridge of ashes." Thus, none of the people whose deaths the aliens engineered are really lost; Archimedes, Julian, Rousseau, Condorcet, da Vinci, the archetypal god-king, and unnamed others all live through the power of the mutant telepathic ability whose evolution the aliens neither foresaw nor forestalled.

Bridge of Ashes would have been impossible to write without Zelazny's considerable reading in history and biography. His fascination with the "low-budget reincarnations" of biography and autobiography clearly led to the evolution of a novel whose central character experiences in fact what Zelazny did vicariously through his reading. The different historical figures that Dennis contacts are sketched in portraits remarkable for their vividness and economy. Without extensive knowledge of the figures Zelazny chose, this would have been impossible. Nor would they have been as appropriate to his plot. Had Zelazny merely chosen those historical figures whom he personally considered as worthy of emulation, the novel's central conflict between the aliens who would guide humanity to destroy the Earth and itself and those who seek to preserve Earth and the human race would have been unsupported and unbelievable.

Roadmarks is another novel heavily indebted to Zelazny's reading program. The setting for the book is one of the more curious time-travel devices in science fiction; Zelazny envisions time as a superhighway. In an interview with *Locus* in October 1991, Zelazny explains how the idea of the Road through time evolved:

> I got the idea for that book during an automobile drive. I was coming up I-25, which is a nice modern highway in New Mexico, and just on a whim, I turned off at a random turnoff I'd never taken before. I drove along for awhile, and I saw a road which was much less kept up. I turned onto that one, and later on I hit a dirt road and I tried it, and pretty soon I came to a place that wasn't on the map. It was just a little settlement. There were log cabins there, and horses pulling carts, and it looked physically as if I'd driven back into the 19th century. I started to think about the way the road kept changing, and I said, "Gee, that would be neat, to consider time as a superhighway with different turnoffs." I went back and started writing *Roadmarks* that same afternoon.[4]

The two things that unite the wide variety of settings and time periods in *Roadmarks* are the Road itself and the central character, Red Dorakeen. One of the first people Red encounters is Adolf

Hitler. Later, the Marquis de Sade appears as a teacher at a writer's conference in a future far from the eighteenth century, where he had gained notoriety for his specialized writings. A Victorian gentleman who receives a brief cameo is clearly meant to be Jack the Ripper. A nameless crusader who lost his crusade pumps gas in a Roadside rest stop and queries those who stop by about the success of the war that he has cheerfully abandoned.

These historical figures give a certain solidity and reality to the fully fictional characters who travel the Road. Not all of these characters are entirely Zelazny's creations, however. Sundoc is based on the pulp fiction hero, Doc Savage. John is based on Jonathan Sunlight, who was the closest person Doc Savage had to an archenemy. Others, like Strangulena, Mondamay, Timyin Tin, Archie Shellman, and Max, although wholly Zelazny's creations, seem to belong to the pulp tradition of larger-than-life heroes and villains. In a curious twist on literary indebtedness, Zelazny notes that Timyin Tin owes something to Sugata, the character from Zelazny's own *Lord of Light* who proved to be the real Buddha.

Zelazny's reading program not only prepared him to write books solidly grounded in actual history and science but also, as is seen in *Roadmarks*, equipped him to pay homage to the literary works that influenced him. The widest area from which he draws his material is, of course, the vast body of myth and legend, which he has used repeatedly to shape the settings of both his science fiction and fantasy works. Although both science fiction and fantasy had used mythological and legendary materials before the 1960s, the usual sources were the myths of classical Greece and Rome, the Norse, and some Celtic, especially those relating to Arthurian material. Zelazny, however, chose to avoid these for the most part and to draw on less familiar traditions.

Zelazny's foundations in mythology are older than the self-education program discussed above. As Zelazny explains in the essay "Fantasy and Science Fiction: A Writer's View," collected in *Frost and Fire*: "My first independent reading as a schoolboy involved mythology – in large quantities. It was not until later that I discovered folk tales, fairy tales, and fantastic voyages. And it was not until considerably later – at age eleven – that I read my first science fiction story."[5] Although mythology began as a "schoolboy" interest, Zelazny never stopped reading in the area: "Most of my mythological background came from primary sources in my earlier years – & later it was Frazer & anthropological sources" (letter, 19 August 1989). In the mid-1980s he began to read Joseph Campbell, starting with the *Masks of God*, *The Hero with a Thousand Faces*, and *Myths to Live By*. Considering both his interest and grounding in mythology, Zelazny's decision to base a large number of his early short stories and novels in a mythological context is unsurprising. A very significant source for this early reading in mythology and legend was Thomas Bulfinch's various collections of legends and myths. The characters encountered on these pages would appear and reappear in various shapes and forms in a wide variety of Zelazny's works. Certainly, a reader familiar with Bulfinch's account of the traitorous Ganelon in *The Legends of Charlemagne* is not surprised to find that Ganelon is the name of the man whom Corwin of Amber remembers as betraying him. Another fine correspondence between legend and fictional character occurs with the son of Brand of Amber. Brand's son is named Rinaldo (although in the books he is more usually referred to by his alias, Luke). Like the Rinaldo of legend, Luke is a valiant and heroic figure who uses his abilities for a wide variety of allies. Also, like the Rinaldo of legend, when faced with deciding what cause he will serve, Luke chooses to serve with those to whom he is bound by both personal and public loyalties.

Although for his first novel, *This Immortal*, Zelazny borrowed primarily from Greek myth, the material he chose to emphasize was not what readers were familiar with from the *Iliad*, *Odyssey*, and other often-read classical texts. Instead, he associated Conrad with the little-known folk legend of the kallikanzaros. The other allusions, while more familiar, take on a different cast in a universe that has to deal with the fey and unpredictable kallikanzaroi rather than the powerful and domineering Olympians.

The Dream Master, especially in its novel form, is almost too heavily allusive. Zelazny intermixes material from the British legend of the ill-fated lovers Tristram and Isolde with the Norse myth of Ragnarok, the end of the world. These tales are not completely compatible, coming as they do from two different cultural views and widely separated time periods. Yet this very lack of congruity is what keeps *The Dream Master* from becoming a mere retelling of the legend of Tristram and Isolde in a different era. The intertwining of the Ragnarok material with the legendary love story makes Charles

Render's fate all the more bleak, for the reader is left with the sense that Render's mental collapse is closer akin to the end of the world than to the romantic insanity of clichéd legend.

With *Lord of Light*, published in 1967, Zelazny departed from the source materials commonly used in science fiction up to that point by incorporating Hindu and Buddhist mythology. The novel was not an attempt to accurately recreate either Hindu or Buddhist culture in another setting. Zelazny's "deicrats" have merely adopted the Hindu pantheon as most fitting for the roles they assume as gods who regularly choose to incarnate in various bodies, changing appearance and even sex at a whim. Sam's decision to resurrect Buddhism does not rest on any belief in its creed but on his perception that it will provide the logical influence to undermine the Hindu-based deicrats. Although Zelazny did not plan on accurately duplicating either Hindu or Buddhist society, he did read extensively before constructing his versions of both traditions. Some of the books he consulted include *The Upanishads*, translated by Swami Nikhilananda; *The Wonder That Was India* by A. L. Basham; *Gods, Demons, and Others* by R. K. Narayan; *Buddhist Texts Through the Ages*, edited by E. Conze; and *Buddha and the Gospel of Buddhism* by Ananda Coomaraswamy.

Creatures of Light and Darkness is another book heavily indebted to Zelazny's readings in mythology. *Creatures* is a curious novel in that it was written without any plans for publication. As Zelazny explains in the foreword to *Bridge of Ashes*, this was:

> my only novel to date written solely for my own amusement, with no expectation that it would ever see print. I have Samuel R. Delany to thank for mentioning its existence to a sympathetic editor. I threw everything but the Egyptian kitchen sink into that book – surrealistic images, a horde of mythological figures, chapters written in free verse and even one done as a closet drama.

Although *Creatures* uses many figures from Egyptian mythology, as in *Lord of Light*, Zelazny's interest is not to duplicate any particular figure or theme from his source material but to use the myths as a starting point from which he constructs his own story. The reader who expects Thoth, Horus, Osiris, Anubis, Isis, or Set to behave somewhat predictably, as their counterparts might in available mythological texts, will be sorely disappointed, but those who read

merely with an ear for the resonances with the myths will find plenty
to satisfy them.

Zelazny drew not only on mythology for the foundations of his
novels, but on those works within the existing body of science fiction
and fantasy. Dilvish, the hero of *Dilvish the Damned* and *The Changing Land*, may owe something to Fritz Leiber's Gray Mouser. The
strange mutating house that is the center of the action in *The Changing Land* is itself a piece of literary homage to William Hope
Hodgson's horror classic *House on the Borderland*. Zelazny acknowledges his debt quite openly, by naming one of the wizards that
Dilvish encounters Hodgson. *The Changing Land* also contains
several references to the works of Hodgson's contemporary H. P.
Lovecraft. The creature imprisoned in the House is referred to as an
"Old One," and certainly resembles the tentacled horrors that Lovecraft so skillfully sketched – despite a capacity for compassion
beyond any of Lovecraft's creatures. Later, the House is threatened
by the Hounds of Thandalos, who emerge from the angles and corner of the rooms in a fashion identical to that of the Hounds of Tin-
dalos, creatures created by Frank Belknap Long in a story of the
same title that has long been associated with Lovecraft's "Cthulhu
Mythos."

Another book that owes a great deal to the older works of science fiction and fantasy is *Nine Princes in Amber*. *Nine Princes*, in a
fashion not shared by the Amber novels that followed it, is heavily
indebted to a short novel, *The Dark World*, by Henry Kuttner.
Zelazny recalls *The Dark World* as "one of my all time childhood
favorites, which appeared in a 1946 issue of *Startling Stories* . . . I
found a used copy a couple of years after its initial appearance, & I
just kept reading it over & over again" (letter, 6 January 1990). The
influence of *The Dark World* on *Nine Princes* is obvious almost from
the opening pages. The story is told as a first-person narrative by a
man named Edward Bond. Bond is haunted by memories of a world
he cannot quite recall. When he is drawn into that world and given
the identity of Ganelon of the Dark World, he does not immediately
become habituated to his new existence. Instead, as the memories of
Ganelon haunted his "twin" Edward Bond, so the memories of
Edward Bond haunt Ganelon, keeping him from fully remembering
who he is and what he must do. The struggle between Ganelon and
Bond to remember is the center of much of the action in *The Dark*

World, for the two men are allied with different sides of a political power struggle. Ganelon, who is power hungry and cruel, is one of the rulers of the Coven. Bond, a World War II veteran pilot, has been one of the leaders of the rebels against the Coven.

The similarity to Zelazny's Corwin of Amber, who struggles throughout the early portion of *Nine Princes* to remember his heritage as a prince of Amber and the reasons for his vendetta against his brothers, is readily apparent. Indeed, the tactics used by the two characters are very similar. In *Nine Princes*, Corwin probes for information, first from his sister Flora, later from his brother Random. He constantly balances the need to discover and the fear of discovery. When Ganelon takes Edward Bond's role among the rebels, his position is nearly identical, although he uses the excuse that a drug has muddled his memory to cover any lapses. Corwin has no "twin" or alternate self, but he is changed enough by his experiences in Shadow that in *Sign of the Unicorn*, one of the later Amber novels, his sister Fiona says: "I have just noticed that this is not really Corwin! It has to be one of his shadows! It has just announced a belief in friendship, dignity, nobility of spirit, and those other things which figure prominently in popular romances!"[6]

Another striking similarity between the two novels is that both contain a major character named Ganelon. As mentioned above, Zelazny's Ganelon owes a great deal to the figure from the legends of Charlemagnian romance. But Zelazny's Ganelon also owes something to Kuttner's Ganelon. Kuttner's Ganelon is a cruel and haughty man, much like Corwin recalls his former ally becoming. Both men are strongly motivated by a desire for revenge. Kuttner's Ganelon agrees to betray the Coven when he learns that they would have sacrificed him during their Sabbat. Zelazny's Ganelon betrays Corwin when he feels that Corwin has passed him over unjustly for a duchy. Finally, like Kuttner's Ganelon, Zelazny's conceals a secret identity. Kuttner's Ganelon passes for the latter portion of the novel as Edward Bond, fooling Bond's allies to gain his revenge on the Coven. Zelazny's Ganelon is the guise that Oberon, King of Amber, adopts to learn about Corwin and then to gain secret access into Amber. In both cases, the character of Ganelon is associated with treachery and shifting identity.

Zelazny has stated that the concept of Amber came to him as a device for investigating a series of parallel realities:

The "Amber" books are a comment on the nature of reality and people's perceptions of it. I was thinking of Lawrence Durrell's "Alexandria Quartet" when I began the first book. I liked that particular series just because of the way he retold the same story from different characters' viewpoints. His was a more general comment on the fact that you can't know everything. He could as easily have written a fifth book or sixth book and kept changing it. That spilled over into the Shadow Worlds and oceans on the different parallel worlds where things are just a little bit different and eventually you get further away and they're a lot different. ("Forever Amber," 5)

Interestingly, despite Zelazny's acknowledged debt to Durrell's work, Kuttner's *The Dark World* is also based on the concept of parallel universes. As is explained to Bond/Ganelon: "Originally the Dark World and the Earth-world were one, in space and time. Then a decision was made – a very vital decision . . . From that point the time-stream branched."[7] For the Amber books, Zelazny has taken this simple concept much further, but it seems likely that the initial association of parallel worlds with the character of Corwin may have its roots in this childhood favorite of Zelazny.

Another similarity between the two works is the liberal sprinkling of references to mythological figures. Kuttner refers to Medea, Llyr, Valkerie, and the Norns as well as a host of more generic legends and myths. Like Zelazny's Amber, the Dark World is the source for many of the legends and myths of Earth. One scene in *The Dark World* nicely illustrates the similar use of allusion by Zelazny and Kuttner. Ganelon/Bond has lifted the harp that will wake a dreaming sorcerer; before he plays it, he reflects:

That harp had been in the Earth-world, or others like it. Legends know its singing strings, as legends tell of mystic swords. There was the lyre of Orpheus, strong with power, that Jupiter placed among the stars. There was the harp of Gwydion of Britain, that charmed the souls of men. And the harp of Alfred, that helped to crush Daneland. There was David's harp that he played before Saul. (Kuttner, 92-93)

In the Ambers, Zelazny refers to some of the same figures from mythology, shaping them to his own purpose. But stronger than any specific correspondence is the idea that the force of events in one world can be powerful enough to create legends in another.

Zelazny's literary homage is not limited to science fiction and fantasy. Collected under the title *My Name Is Legion* are three shorter works: "The Eve of RUMOKO," " 'Kjwalll'kje'k'koothailll-'kje'k," and "Home is the Hangman." These feature the same protagonist, a nameless troubleshooter who has gone out of his way to make certain that he is not listed in the world data bank. Thus, officially he does not exist. This makes him ideal for certain types of jobs. Zelazny considers the character a tribute to the Travis McGee stories of John D. MacDonald. Both his nameless character and McGee have found ways to cut free from the restrictions of their society (McGee is independently wealthy and lives on a boat). Both use their freedom to take the jobs that for one reason or another governments or official organizations cannot. Both, therefore, are a last resort for those who hire them. The difficulties that Zelazny's nameless character finds himself in are more outlandish, but the similarity between the two characters is strong.

Another short piece written as a deliberate literary homage is "A Museum Piece." Here Zelazny does a take-off of John Collier's story "Evening Primrose." Zelazny's setting is different, a museum rather than a department store, just as his hero is a sculptor rather than a poet. The essential character motivations and plot elements are the same, however. Another debt Zelazny may owe to Collier is in the development of Mary Maude Mullen, the Victorian doyenne of the Set in Zelazny's *The Graveyard Heart*. Mary Maude Mullen closely resembles the eerie, nearly transparent Mrs. Vanderpants, ruler of the strange crew who live in Bracey's Giant Emporium in Collier's story.

Perhaps the most ambitious piece of literary homage in Zelazny's canon to this point is the novel *The Black Throne*, written in collaboration with fellow science fiction author Fred Saberhagen. The initial idea for the novel occurred to Saberhagen, a Poe enthusiast. Saberhagen presented his idea to Zelazny, with whom he had already collaborated on the novel *Coils*. Although already familiar with Poe's works, Zelazny read both all of Poe's works and a host of critical works and biographies of the author to prepare for the project. Only when this groundwork was in place did the actual writing begin.

The Black Throne is a strange tale told by the first-person narrator, Edgar Allan Perry. As all Poe aficionados know, Edgar Perry is the pseudonym that Poe used when he enlisted in the military. The novel begins with Perry (Poe), and a girl named Annie meeting in a world that may be Annie's dream. As the children grow into adulthood, their meetings become less and less frequent. The novel comes to focus on Perry's quest to rescue Annie when she is kid-napped. What makes the novel particularly fascinating is that the landscape through which Perry journeys is shaped by and peopled from the stories and poems written by Edgar Allan Poe.

This attention to the details from Poe's fiction is both the novel's its greatest strength and greatest weakness. At times the plot seems contrived and convoluted to make it fit within the strictures set by Poe's stories. Annie, the woman who is so compelling to Perry that he will pursue her through deadly peril, is never really developed. She remains a victim awaiting rescue through most of the story. Perry is also somewhat flat – a classic hero but little more. Still, the secondary characters drawn from Poe's fiction are often beautifully done. Of particular interest are Dirk Peters (from *The Strange Narrative of A. Gordon Pym*) and his orangutan, who accompany Perry through much of his journey. Overshadowing everything in the novel is the powerful, haunted figure of Poe himself. Caught in nightmares, madness, and alcoholism, the poet and author dreams of a world that he knows is out of his reach and that by its unattainable existence drives him to despair. In the end, one feels as if the real challenge were faced not by Perry but by Poe and that, sadly, Poe has lost.

Collaboration

Saberhagen is not the only author with whom Zelazny has collabo-rated. To this date, Zelazny has written eight novels in partnership with other authors, and a short story with Harlan Ellison. These authors include, in addition to Saberhagen, Philip K. Dick, Robert Sheckley, Thomas T. Thomas, and Gerald Hausman. Zelazny states that his central reason for writing collaborations is that it extends his knowledge of the writing process and forces him to stretch his own skills. Zelazny gives a fine example of how this worked when he did his first collaboration on *Deus Irae* with Philip K. Dick. In this case, Zelazny came into the project when Dick had started the novel but was unable to complete it:

> Before I'd started on it, I read or re-read sufficient of his material to teach my-self how to mimic his style. I didn't do it, though, but chose a style partway be-

tween his & mine, a kind of meta-Phil Dick style which blended well [with] his own & made the thing come out sounding like something reminiscent of both of us but not exactly like either. (letter, 3 August 1989)

Most of the other collaborations have begun in a more deliberate fashion. Usually, Zelazny chooses to work with authors he knows well and admires already for some element of their craft. An example of this is Robert Sheckley, with whom Zelazny has collaborated to date on two novels: *Bring Me the Head of Prince Charming* and *If at Faust You Don't Succeed*. Zelazny said of Sheckley as their collaboration was first developing:

Bob was a masterful short story writer whom I admired greatly back before I became a pro myself . . . [he] has done an awful lot of reading throughout his life. His background in literature & philosophy overlaps mine a good deal, even in some fairly obscure areas. (letter, 15 May 1989)

While the subject matter of *Bring Me the Head of Prince Charming* was developed from a desire to do a humorous parody of various fairy tale conventions, *If at Faust You Don't Succeed* grew from the serious interest of both authors in the various Faust legends. Quite likely as the authors continue to collaborate, their fascination for twisting and stretching recognized legend lore will remain central to their plots.

Zelazny's collaboration with Harlan Ellison on "Come to Me Not in Winter's White" originated by Ellison's request. Ellison's introduction to the story describes in detail the method by which the story was written. Zelazny wrote the opening, as Ellison notes, "writing through to the paragraph whose last line is *Still he worked to slow her room even more,* and then mailing the pages to me. He did not indicate where or how he thought the story should go, as he had assumed the role of picking the game, and it was my job to set the rules."[8] Zelazny and Ellison wrote alternate sections of about 1,000 words each, taking turns developing the characters and plot complications. Ellison ends his introduction to the story by commenting, in a similar vein to Zelazny's reflections, that collaborations allow a writer to expand as an artist:

In a career lifetime of writing violent and frequently loveless fictions, this is one of the few times I feel my work has reached toward gentleness and compassion, and I don't think I would have been able to do anything even remotely like it, had it not been for Roger. It also introduced me to the writings of Pablo Neruda, and if I'd been enriched no further, it would have been worth it. (454)

Only one of Zelazny's collaborations did not begin with an established social/professional relationship as the basis. Zelazny was already acquainted with Thomas T. Thomas before they began work on *The Mask of Loki*, but the collaboration was encouraged by editor Jim Baen, who felt that they would work well together. Zelazny did enjoy working with Thomas, and after the completion of their first work almost immediately began work with him on a second book, *Flare*. Like Zelazny, Thomas has been praised for his creative, somewhat quirky protagonists and settings. He is also a quite skilled writer, with a talent for both stylistic flourishes and occasional outbursts of poetic language. An interesting note is that while for *The Mask of Loki* Zelazny suggested the quotations from Omar Khayyam, Thomas came up with the quotations from more modern sources (from Shakespeare through Dylan Thomas) that head the alternate chapters.

Although the majority of Zelazny's collaborations have been in the science fiction or fantasy area, *Wilderness*, originally titled *Colter/Glass*, written with Gerald Hausman, is a tale of two diverse yet parallel psychological quests both based on historical people and events. The "Colter" in the title refers to Samuel Colter, who discovered Yellowstone Park (then called "Colter's Hell"). "Glass" is famous mountain man Hugh Glass, whose story is told in the American epic poem "Song of Hugh Glass" by John G. Neihardt.

Fiction Writing

One of the reasons Zelazny enjoys learning from other writers through collaboration is that, like many professional writers, Zelazny never studied fiction writing formally. He says: "All my thinking, all my conclusions as to how it's done came after the fact. At first, I just sat down and started writing" (letter, 25 February 1990). Zelazny's awareness of the terminology of writing came not from studying it but from teaching it. One anecdote beautifully illustrates this:

I remember once teaching at a writers' conference in Indiana where they'd hired Phyllis Eisenstein (who *had* studied it) to be my assistant. At one point, where I was talking about avoiding the common mistake of introducing a long expository digression near the story's beginning, & of turning the withholding of that information into a virtue by using the absence of information to create some mystery, & then doling it out slowly amidst action as a reward rather than an exercise in boredom, I paused & asked for questions. When I'd answered all of those from the class, Phyllis suggested I explain how that practice actually goes all the way back to the narrative hook. I recall thinking about it as hard as I could for several seconds, then finally asking her, "Okay, what the hell's a narrative hook?" She thought I was joking. I wasn't. I'd been writing professionally for something like 12 years at that point. (letter, 25 February 1990)

From this experience, Zelazny decided to add another element to his reading program. First, he learned the terminology commonly used by writing instructors, then he established the practice of reading a book on the subject of writing before going to teach at a conference or workshop. In this way, he keeps current with both the vocabulary and the trends.

A final literary area in which Zelazny has cultivated an interest is children's literature. Among his own works are three books intended for younger readers: *Here There Be Dragons*, *Way Up High*, and *A Dark Travelling*. *Doorways in the Sand* has also been marketed for young adults, although it was not written with that particular audience in mind. Zelazny's interest in the area grows from his own enthusiasm for such works. This interest was reawakened by Andre Norton, who convinced him to read several E. Nesbit works when she learned that he had missed them as a child. Zelazny still regularly reads works of fiction written for young adults; particular favorites are the contemporary gothic novels of John Bellairs and Susan Cooper's "Dark Is Rising" series.

His interest goes beyond the enjoyment of a good story, however. He is also a student of the different approach involved when crafting a book for a nonadult audience. A book that has been particularly influential in shaping his opinions on the subject is *The Green and Burning Tree: On the Writing and Enjoyment of Children's Books* by Eleanor Cameron. Zelazny views Cameron's thesis about time in children's literature as very persuasive. As Zelazny sees it, Cameron's thesis is that "the very best of children's literature is a form of fantasy [with] something of an Eastern philosophical view of

Time rather than a linear Western way of looking at it" (letter, 13 May 1989). Another favorite critical work in the area is *Don't Tell the Grownups* by Alison Lurie, with its mixing of biography and criticism on a range of popular children's authors.

As is obvious when reading Zelazny's own works written for a younger audience, the approach he takes is not markedly different from the one he takes when writing for adults. The vocabulary may be somewhat simpler, the technical material explained in a bit more detail, but otherwise Zelazny adheres to the tradition that maintains that works written for younger readers do not necessarily need to teach, preach, or talk down to that audience. Written in such a fashion, Zelazny's "children's books" are accessible to all of his readers, no matter what their age.

Although literature and literary arts form an important portion of Zelazny's reading program, an essential nonliterary area is his reading in the sciences. Zelazny's interest in ecology has already been discussed but, as might be expected of a science fiction writer, Zelazny has kept himself educated on the developments in a wide variety of sciences, both hard and soft. Although, as in history and literature, he uses the "key book" concept to develop his knowledge of scientific matters, in Zelazny's earlier works his own experience often shaped the subject matter with which he chose to work.

Sciences

Psychology, as noted earlier, was Zelazny's first choice as an undergraduate major. Even after he had switched to English, his interest in the field remained. This interest continually crops up in his fiction. Perhaps the most obvious example is the early novella "He Who Shapes," which was later expanded into the novel *The Dream Master*. Render, the story's protagonist, is a psychiatrist whose consulting couch has been replaced by the futuristic "ro-womb," which enables him to enter into and shape patients' fantasies.

This combination of the "soft" science of psychology with harder technological improvements is not unique to *The Dream Master*. In one of his contributions to the much lighter Wild Card series, Zelazny once again combines psychology and technology. In Zelazny's story "Concerto for Siren and Serotonin" from *Wild Cards V: Down and Dirty*, Zelazny's character Croyd Crenson is helped to fall peacefully asleep without drugs by use of a device for brain wave entrainment and suggestion. In the comic book atmosphere of the Wild Cards shared universe, where heroes can fly through the air like Superman and villains change into monsters straight from grade B movies, this "brain wave entrainment" could be passed off as just another bit of fictional science. As Dr. Finn tells Croyd, however, brain wave entrainment has been under investigation for years. According to Zelazny, a device similar to the one Finn uses on Croyd exists today and is being used to explore various theories of how the abilities of the human brain might be developed and enhanced.

In "The Long Sleep," Zelazny's story for *Wild Cards XIII: Card Sharks*, a psychiatrist is again a major character. Although Dr. Pan Rudo is technically a villain, this does not make his grounding in psychology shoddy. Rudo is a neuropsychiatrist who has studied with Freud and at the Jungian Institute. His field of interest is "dauerschlaff," the study of the relationship between sleep and the ability of the mind and body to heal. This, of course, makes him of great interest to Croyd, whom the Wild Card virus has mutated so that whenever he falls asleep his entire body – including appearance, sex, and any "talents" – is open to change. At one point in the story, there is a long discourse on the various psychological theories that Rudo has drawn from to develop his own. Rudo's own theory, not surprisingly, mingles material from both psychology and literature. As Croyd explains:

> He felt that life is a compromise between what you want and what you get, and that there's always fear involved in the transaction . . . He said that we tell ourselves lies in order to deal with it . . . He had this idea, actually, from the playwright Ibsen, who called the big one – the big phony construct about yourself and the world – a "life lie."[9]

Zelazny's mingling of psychological theory and literature enables him to create a reasonable explanation both for Croyd's condition and for Pan Rudo's ability to cure him without being able, necessarily, to cure the other victims of the Wild Card virus – a plot complication that could effectively terminate the series.

Several of Zelazny's "harder" science fiction stories have their roots in the same mixture of experience and self-education as those stories that rely on his training in psychology. When Zelazny enlisted in the Ohio National Guard his initial training was with Nike Ajax guided missiles; later the guard switched to the Nike Hercules system and Zelazny was transferred to the 112th Engineers Battalion, where he learned to drive an armored vehicle launch bridge. Zelazny noted that " 'neutral steer' . . . which makes one tread go one way & the other the other way, thus spinning the thing around" was used in his short story "Devil Car" (letter, 28 October 1989). Certainly, his work with tanks influenced the design and function of the heavily armored vehicles in several stories, including "Devil Car," "Last of the Wild Ones," *Damnation Alley*, and *Lord of Light*.

Zelazny does not need to have a personal foundation in a science to employ that science in his writings, however. *Lord of Light* combines Zelazny's strength in mythology and characterization with a wealth of more or less probable scientific devices ranging from cryonics, body tanks, thought transfer, and a wealth of futuristic trinkets and weapons. The concept for *Flare*, which traces the passage of a solar flare in a fashion similar to the way George R. Stewart traced the life of a hurricane in *Storm*, developed from Zelazny's interest in solar astronomy.

Currently, with virtual reality a growing interest in both the computer science and the science fiction areas, one can easily forget that the concept is neither newly invented nor newly explored. Reviewing the course of Zelazny's writings, one can see that he was using virtual reality as early as *The Dream Master*. *Coils*, written in collaboration with Fred Saberhagen, expands the idea of an interrelationship between human perceptions and computer-created realities. Kit, in "24 Views of Mount Fugi by Hokusai," has abandoned his human body for the freedom and power offered by a worldwide computer matrix. Thus, in his recent "Donnerjack of Virtu" books, Zelazny is not joining a current trend of fascination with the potential of a developing scientific field but is continuing along an area of interest that he has been developing for decades.

Whatever the material he is studying, whether science or literature or anything in between, the thing that provides an overarching structure is Zelazny's fascination with the craft of writing itself:

> I find writing almost as fascinating from the observer's standpoint as from the creator's. I am always amazed at how it can be calibrated. Look at someone like Keats, or Radiguet, or Rimbaud. If one is too young to be packed full of experience or information one can make a go of it at the lyric level, capitalizing on one's expressive abilities. Or look at Wodehouse, writing in his 90s, all

of it springing from his sense of humor. While I do not believe that it is best for an established writer always to write from strength, I do feel that it is the best tactic for a beginning writer to find her strong points . . . I have always believed that whatever one possesses will be sufficient to the task if one considers it well & applies one's abilities ingeniously. (letter, 18 May 1989)

Certainly, one can see that Zelazny has done precisely this with his own works and educational development and that he has built from his initial stylistic strength to works more heavily based in substance. As he has continued writing, his works have been influenced by the information that he has accumulated through his reading program. The reader does not need to share his knowledge to enjoy his writings. As Zelazny himself has stated: "My intent has long been to write stories that can be read in many ways from the simple to the complex. I feel that they must first be enjoyable simply as stories . . . even for one who can't catch *any* of the allusions" (letter, 5 June 1990). Judging from the continuing interest shown in his works by a wide variety of readers, Zelazny is succeeding admirably in balancing accessibility and allusion.

Chapter Three

The Arts – Visual, Musical, Martial – and Place as Inspiration

Perhaps not as simple to trace, but as important as Zelazny's education and subsequent reading program, is the influence of various nonliterary interests on Zelazny's writing. These include his interest in arts and in music, his participation in a variety of martial arts, and his relocation to New Mexico and subsequent fascination with the cultural mix of the area.

Art

Zelazny's enthusiasm for art in many forms, but perhaps especially the graphic arts, had its beginning when he was a boy: "I remember reading newspaper comic strips & editorial cartoons as soon as I began to read. Then comic books, along [with] regular reading. I never stopped enjoying the comics. I'm a fan of comic art & I enjoy good commercial art" (letter, 13 May 1992). Comic art has retained its appeal for Zelazny in part because of the stylized naturalism often used by artists in that particular form. Zelazny's early interest in comics has led him to deliberately seek occasions throughout his career when his written text could be enhanced by the addition of a visual component.

One of his earliest efforts to do this was around late 1969, when he solicited Vaughn Bode to illustrate his children's books *Way Up High* and *Here There Be Dragons*. Ironically, the books would not see press until 1992, partly because of complications resulting from the processing of Vaughn Bode's estate after his death in 1974. Zelazny admired Bode's work, and when he recalled that Bode was fond of drawing reptiles he decided to approach Bode about the possibility of illustrating the stories – one of which features a pterodactyl and the other a dragon. Bode agreed, and the resulting illustrations beautifully complement Zelazny's stories.

Bode's style for both of the pieces relies mostly on soft, curving lines and distorted proportions that use exaggeration for emphasis. Suzie, the little girl in *Way Up High*, has enormous eyes and thick hair that falls past her waist. Both of these traits conspire to make her especially diminutive without becoming fragile – the perfect depiction of a girl who would cross-examine a pterodactyl one moment and go off riding on his back the next. No effort is made to make the pterodactyl anything except a large, rather ugly brown lizard, but Bode's care in drawing the creature's expressions, especially the eyes, hints at the secret that is at the heart of this bittersweet tale.

For *Here There Be Dragons*, Bode draws with especially fine attention to detail. That the map on the desk of Mister Gibberling, the cartographer, be carefully worked out seems only reasonable, since the cartographer's tendency to distort what he does not know is at the heart of the story, but Bode beautifully characterizes Gibberling through his cracked monocle, frayed quill pen, and even the dripping candle wax on the overburdened fixture over his desk. Whereas the colors in *Way Up High* are rich and vivid – so much so that the apples against the dark green leaves of the tree seem to glow – the colors for *Here There Be Dragons* are more muted. Several times, an entire plate is done in shades of one color. Therefore, when a vivid shade is used, as in the plate illustrating the little lizard Bell's transformation into a gigantic dragon, the contrast is as astonishing to the viewer as the event must have been to the guests at the Prince's party. Although the various delays in production mean that both *Way Up High* and *Here There Be Dragons* are in a sense period pieces, both the whimsical stories and their accompanying artwork contain something that transcends the time and style of their making.

Another author whose work Zelazny admires is Jack Gaughan. When Zelazny's first son, Devin, was born in 1971, Zelazny asked Gaughan to design the birth announcement. For the 1974 Worldcon, a souvenir booklet containing some of Zelazny's poetry was compiled and illustrated by Gaughan. The stark, stylized black and white drawings provide an eerie counterpart to Zelazny's cryptic free verse. Gaughan does not seek to interpret the poems through his artwork, yet each drawing contains some element easily recognizable from the poem it depicts. Thus, Gaughan succeeds in illustrating without interpreting – a difficult task rarely achieved in similar books. Gaughan also provided both the cover art and the interior illustrations for Zelazny's short story "Unicorn Variation" when it was published in *The Magazine of Fantasy and Science Fiction*. Zelazny had hoped to have him illustrate "24 Views of Mount Fuji by Hokusai," but because of Gaughan's failing health this proved impossible.

In 1978 Zelazny entered into another project with an artist – *The Illustrated Roger Zelazny* – this time with Gray Morrow. Unlike the previous illustrated works, this volume involved more collaboration between artist and writer and, as the introduction to the volume notes, *The Illustrated Roger Zelazny* was something innovative for the time: "What you hold in your hand is nothing less than a ground-breaking experiment in graphic science fiction. Each of the five fantasies in this book are developed in a different way. At least two systems of graphic storytelling have never been seen before in this country."[1] Certainly, the book was a successful experiment, going through several different editions and becoming the first graphic story collection to be selected by the Science Fiction Book Club.

The book contains several previously published Zelazny pieces: "A Rose for Ecclesiastes," "The Doors of His Face, the Lamps of His Mouth," "The Furies," and "Rock Collector" (based on the short story "Collector's Fever"). Each of these stories is "adapted" (that is, shortened) with Zelazny's consent to allow for more visual space. The book also includes both "An Amber Tapestry: Epic Murals Based on Corwin and the Amber Worlds" and "A Zelazny Tapestry: Key Scenes from the Zelazny Novels." The majority of the artwork is in color, with "The Doors of His Face, the Lamps of His Mouth" and "Rock Collector" in black and white.

The book also includes an original short story, "Shadowjack," which uses the character of Jack of Shadows from Zelazny's book of that title. Zelazny notes that a trading of ideas went on as the story was developed:

Gray Morrow had wanted badly to do something [with] Jack of Shadows, as he liked the character, so he told me some things he'd like to draw. I cobbled them together into this prequel's story-line, he laid out the [pages] for it in rough, then I went back & wrote the continuity to match his sequence of [illustrations] (letter, 21 February 1990)

The fashion in which "Shadowjack" was composed made it more than just an artist illustrating a writer, but a joint composition between the two.

The 1979 Ace edition of *The Illustrated Roger Zelazny* omits "Rock Collector" and prints much of the original color art in a smaller size and/or in black and white, reducing much of the impact of Morrow's contribution. Morrow's text in the "Morrow Speaks" section is cut to a few lines that unfortunately omit his reflections on the growing interrelations among various media in science fiction. Finally, captions are provided for "Amber Tapestry."

Overall, Morrow's illustrations provide a successful treatment of Zelazny's works. Zelazny says he "was impressed by the fact that [Morrow] changed his style of illustration for each piece" (letter, 21 February 1990). To a careful reader, however, there are some curious incongruities between the text and the pictures. Braxa, whose mouth is described in the text as "the red wound in that pale, pale cameo, her face," is usually drawn with her lips painted blue or green. The giant Siamese cats in "Amber Tapestry" resemble bearded pumas. Corwin's sisters are done in such a generic fashion as to be almost unidentifiable. One caption identifies the picture as Fiona, Flora, and Llewella, but none of the ladies presented has Fiona's characteristic fiery red hair. Such comments, however, are really quibbling over minutia. The collaboration of Morrow and Zelazny not only provided a very enjoyable text but also helped to create what has become an accepted and appreciated development in science fiction and fantasy writing.

About 10 years after the appearance of *The Illustrated Roger Zelazny*, Zelazny again collaborated on a text that focused on illustrations of his work. *Roger Zelazny's Visual Guide to Castle Amber* was a more complicated project than the earlier work, involving the participation of another writer, Neil Randall, two artists, Todd Cameron Hamilton and Jim Clouse, and Bill Fawcett as an organizer. Neil Randall's introduction provides a charming description of the four-day process of collecting the information for the *Visual Guide*:

Todd Hamilton and Jim Clouse peppered him with question after interminable question about Castle Amber itself, and later about the art of the Trumps. Bill

Fawcett, who organized it all, extracted even more information. I sat in the corner, reading the as-yet-unreleased *Sign of Chaos*. It was an honor, and I won't easily forget it.

And with each new question Roger Zelazny would stop, and raise his hands, and then put them back down and let the words pour forth. Often he would close his eyes as he talked, recalling every last detail about the world he created – or perhaps discovered – over the course of eight extremely popular novels. Sometimes he would hesitate, as if unwilling to tell us some Amberian secret, but in the end he would relent, and let us know what he was thinking about. Those thoughts – always – confirmed his belief in his world. Then we all began writing and drawing.[2]

The *Visual Guide* is presented as a tour of Castle Amber conducted by Flora, one of the Princesses of Amber. The visual component consists of two parts: maps and paintings. The detailed maps of the castle, both overall and room by room, are done by James Clouse. Clouse provides more than mere line drawing showing locations relative to one another. He goes as far as drawing in the details of furnishing and decor in each room so that they match the text precisely. Sometimes these details become whimsical, such as an unmade bed or a pile of papers left on a table. Thus, the drawings are as much illustrations as they are maps.

The excellent detail of Clouse's maps, however, is often overshadowed by the strangely beautiful paintings of Todd Cameron Hamilton. The *Visual Guide* is done completely in black and white, but the lack of color does not appear to have restricted Hamilton at all. Most of the pictures have a silky silver texture; when darker colors are used, as in the picture of booted feet walking the Pattern on page 181 or the storm hound on page 197, the contrast to the gentler shades of the other pictures makes their impact all the more noticeable. Hamilton's paintings fall into two categories: those illustrating various scenes or items of Amber and the Greater Trumps.

The Trumps in the *Visual Guide* are much more complete than those in Morrow's "Amber Tapestry," not only because they include characters from later books but also because they include the female members of the royal family. Each Trump began as a large, 18"-by-30" painting; in the book they are reduced to 4" by 7". The format of each Trump is similar. The outer border of the majority of the Trumps is an intricate design containing a chess rook, swords, a pocket watch, and flowers intertwined with vines. In the top border

of each card, set within a diamond-shaped border, is a serene ar-
chaic face; at the bottom is a matching face, its expression in a fierce
grimace. Curiously, on the Trump for Luke/Rinaldo the side borders
are reversed. In the corners of each Trump is the device of the person pictured; for example, a shooting star for Brand, a dolphin for
Llewella, a phoenix for Luke, and, of course, a silver rose for Corwin.
Interestingly, the devices for Martin and Merlin are so abstract as to
tell virtually nothing about the person, perhaps reflecting the idea
that neither of these young men has fully defined himself.

In a conversation at the 1989 Lunacon, Hamilton noted that the
Trumps were designed from Zelazny's verbal descriptions, augmented by the descriptions from the various novels. Often he would
do a quick sketch based on the details that Zelazny would provide
and then show it to Zelazny, who would comment and offer alterations as necessary. Thus, perhaps more so than any other set of
Trumps, Hamilton's reflect Zelazny's image of the Amberites. When
the book was completed, Hamilton made a gift to Zelazny of the
Trump of Benedict.

In the early 1990s, a fairly large concentration of illustrated
Zelazny works appeared. As mentioned above, the two children's
books illustrated by Vaughn Bode finally saw publication in summer
1992. The first of the Amber Graphic novels produced by Marvel with
art by Lou Harrison and script by Terry Bisson are planned for 1994.
Harrison met with Zelazny to discuss the project, but most of the
work was done independently, with Zelazny sending various design
proofs along the way. The text is, of course, abridged, but Hartman's
creative depictions of characters and scenes effectively replace long
passages of descriptive prose.

There is nothing cartoonish about Harrison's style. He uses light
and shadow as carefully as if he were drawing portraits from life. He
is especially clever with background details, such as the changes to
Flora's car as Random and Corwin shadow-shift their way back to
Amber. Julian's storm hounds are also beautifully done; their narrow
skulls and toothy jaws emphasize as neatly as any prose text that
their master has created them to hunt and kill and for nothing else.
He does take liberty with minor details, such as transforming the an-
tique cavalry saber over Flora's mantel into a Japanese katana.

Harrison's interpretation alters the descriptions of the Amberites
somewhat, but the changes do not violate the essential personality of

the character. Flora, for example, is depicted as a redhead rather than a blond. Random, when Corwin meets him on the Shadow Earth, resembles a modern MTV rocker rather than a down-at-the-heels jazz drummer. One major liberty Harrison does take with Zelazny's description is that of Corwin in Amber. Corwin, on both his Trump and in the Shadows proximate to Amber, is depicted with a heavy, rather shaggy beard, although Zelazny clearly indicates that he is clean-shaven. This alteration from the prose text does, however, permit the artist to make a rather striking contrast between those scenes set on Earth and those in Amber.

Smaller circulation items include a limited edition portfolio of paintings based on Zelazny's Amber series by artist Lew Hartman, planned for publication in March 1993. The *Amber* role-playing game and its associated magazine *Amberzine* also provided opportunities for illustrations inspired by the Amber books to reach a wider audience than the more informal fan circles.

Perhaps the most fascinating of Zelazny's more recent collaborations is the novel *A Night in the Lonesome October* illustrated by Gahan Wilson, published in August 1993. The idea for the novel came to Zelazny as early as 1979, but Wilson was not available to illustrate the story. Zelazny put the idea in a back file and forgot about it until December 1991, when he came across the notes and the story began to haunt him. (As mentioned elsewhere, Zelazny often describes the characters in his stories as ghosts, and his novels are often character driven.) He started writing *October* in mid-December and completed a first draft by March. This time Wilson was available, and the project immediately became a reality.

The illustrations in *October* are the sinuous, grotesque black and white line drawings for which Wilson is so well-known. With his drawings for *October*, Wilson has achieved the remarkable feat of illustrating the story in precise detail without giving away anything that would give away the plot. This alone would be a worthy achievement, but Wilson also manages to capture the tone of whimsical horror that dominates Zelazny's text without once becoming cute or reductive.

Not all of Zelazny's collaborations have begun with the story first and the art second. Early in his writing career, he was repeatedly hired by *Galaxy* to write stories around a previously purchased piece of cover art. "The Man Who Loved the Faoli," "Angel, Dark

Angel," and "He That Moves" were all written in this fashion. So was
"The Song of the Blue Baboon," a story with which Zelazny was less
than pleased and which, oddly, was published separately from the
cover originally planned.

Another story that had its birth in the prospect of a union of
visual and written elements is the novel *Changeling*. Zelazny was approached by Nelvana studios in Toronto, Canada, about the possibility of writing a story that could later be adapted for animation.
Zelazny wrote *Changeling* with this in mind, trying for highly visual
metaphors. Thus, Pol Detson, the protagonist, perceives magical
energy in the form of brightly colored lines that he weaves and ties
to create the desired effect. Other mages see their power differently,
but equally visually. Ibal perceives it as swarming lights, like insects;
Keth sees it as balls of colored light. Later, Pol grows beyond his
early limitations, but even his more sophisticated magic remains
highly pictorial. Although the project with Nelvana studios did not
materialize, both *Changeling* and its sequel *Madwand* were released
with illustrations; *Changeling*'s were done by Estaban Maroto and
Madwand's by Judy King Rieniets. Zelazny did not contribute to the
artist selection; it was done by editor Jim Baen, who also commissioned the illustrations for the Zelazny and Saberhagen collaboration
Coils.

Zelazny's enthusiasm for art also found its way into his stories in
a form less direct than collaboration. The Isle of the Dead in
Zelazny's novel of that title is taken by Sandow from "that mad
painting by Boecklin, *The Isle of the Dead*."[3] The early short story "A
Museum Piece" tells of a young man who decides to retire from the
world by posing as a piece of sculpture until he meets a young lady
with a similar plan and an alien anthropologist posing as a mobile.
The museum Zelazny set this in was a somewhat rearranged version
of the Cleveland Museum of Art, where he would often go to study
while in college.

"Permafrost," a somewhat later story, contains several references to famous works of art. In the section titled "The Statue,"
Glenda's frozen corpse is described as "looking like one of Rodin's
less comfortable figures" (*Frost*, 21). Various divisions quite deliberately evoke the imagery of Salvador Dali's famous "melted watch"
painting, "The Persistence of Memory":

Those three sections in "Permafrost" which are titled "The Limp Watch Hung Upon the Treelimb," "The Limp Treelimb Hung Upon the Watch," & "Frozen Watch, Imbedded in Permafrost" are references to one of Salvador Dali's most famous paintings – the one [with] the limp watches hanging on the limbs of a tree. The key is the painting's title. It's called "The Persistence of Memory." The reason is that "Permafrost" is – particularly at that point, when my protagonist is headed toward the cave where it all began – a story of memory. (letter, 5 July 1992)

Another use of art in a story occurs within the latter five Amber novels. Merlin and his friend Luke are artists and art collectors. Both of these younger sons of Amber are Trump artists, following in the tradition of their great-grandfather Dworkin. Merlin also enjoys roaming the family art museums in Chaos, which he recalls as some of his favorite playgrounds when he was a child. These artistic leanings help to characterize Merlin as quite different from his sword-swinging, if poetic, father.

An intermingling of Merlin's mundane and magical involvements occurs when he is travelling in the place between Shadows in *Knight of Chaos*. Merlin reaches out through a Shadow interface and finds himself touching a red '57 Chevy that he recognizes, not because he owns the car but because he owns a Polly Jackson painting of the car. In both *Knight of Shadows* and *Prince of Chaos* he summons this not completely natural vehicle to his aid instead of the clichéd war-horse of fantasy literature. Interestingly, Zelazny, rather than Merlin, is the owner of the Polly Jackson painting of the red '57 Chevy (he also owns one of the woodcuts in the Yoshitoshi Mori "Face to Face" series, similar to the one that Eric "borrows" from Corwin). For the August 1992 issue of *Amazing Stories*, which commemorated the thirtieth anniversary of Zelazny's first science fiction publication, editor Kim Mohan commissioned Polly Jackson to illustrate "Passion Play."

An intertextual crossover between Zelazny's interest in graphic art and his own writing occurs in *Blood of Amber* when a man with "a nasty-looking scar running both above and below his left eye" (55) warns Merlin about potential assault by a couple of young thugs. Zelazny has admitted that Old John is a cameo for John Gaunt, also known as Grimjack, the protagonist of one of Zelazny's favorite comics. In 1989, Zelazny provided the introduction for the *Grimjack* graphic novel *Demon Knight*. In this short piece he praises writer

John Ostrander and his collaborating artists for creating a tale that shows how the story-telling process can be enhanced when the visual and the written intertwine.

Over the years, Zelazny has followed a wide variety of titles in addition to *Grimjack*. His current favorites include Hugo Pratt's *Corto Maltese* and Neil Gaiman's *Sandman*. Zelazny's appreciation of Gaiman's works led to his being commissioned to write the introduction for the collected volume of Gaiman's *Books of Magic* in 1992. He is also very fond of political cartoons and is a special fan of the work of Bill Mauldin, two of whose signed, original cartoons hang on the wall of his family room.

Zelazny also collects both science fiction art and art unrelated to the area. One piece of which he is particularly fond is the Hannes Bok illustration for "A Rose for Ecclesiastes." Zelazny was familiar with Bok's earlier works dating back to his own reading in the early pulp magazines. Bok's illustration for Zelazny's now classic story was one of Bok's final pieces before his death. Hanging on the wall to the left of Zelazny's desk, it seems a reminder of the early work in the area that inspired him to follow the path he has chosen. Other works in his collection include Tom Canty's "Flora" (later retitled "Lady Winter"), which Zelazny says is a perfect portrait of that princess of Amber.

Zelazny also collects cards, a hobby that mingles his interest in art and legend. This interest, in turn, had its part in inspiring the design of the Amber Trumps:

> I used to collect playing cards. Had several hundred odd decks (still have many of them, actually), including Tarots. No special set influenced me here, though I'm familiar [with] all of the popular ones & many oddball decks. I've read Catherine Perry Hargraves' HISTORY OF PLAYING CARDS, Roger Tilley's HISTORY OF PLAYING CARDS & Sylvia Mann's COLLECTING PLAYING CARDS. (letter, 24 February 1989)

Zelazny's interest in mythology fueled his interest in the various Tarot systems, although he denies any direct correspondence between his studies in the area and his use of the material in his work:

> Also, I'm familiar [with] various occult interpretations of the Tarots, as I think of occult systems as mini-mythologies & have studied them, also, as part of my general interest in the myth-making process. So, while I can't point to a par-

ticular deck or interpretive system & say that it influenced me, it's possible that it did, anyway. With respect to individual characters, okay, yes, there is some truth to relating the Amberites to the Tarot figures – but there is not an intentional one-for-one overall correspondence anywhere. The cards are more points of departure, here & there, & I'd hate to endorse a psychology of types for the characters based on them. (letter, 24 February 1989)

Unsurprisingly, the Trumps of Amber have inspired a great amount of artwork. Trumps have been presented as marketing tie-ins, as with the French edition of the Ambers and the set designed to go with the *Amber* role-playing game. The Marvel comics graphic novel also shows versions of the Amber Trumps. A set by Christine A. McLaren has been included in an encyclopedia of playing cards. There was even an Amber card game designed in the 1960s by Sadhana, but it was never produced commercially. Amateur artists have produced numerous Trumps of their favorite characters and many times send copies to Zelazny, who often adds them to his own card collection.

Another item that Zelazny collects is oriental rugs. He owns about 30 and a small library of books on the subject. As with anything that fascinates him, the rugs have a way of finding their way into his stories, sometimes just as decoration, other times in ways that affect the action of the story. In *The Hand of Oberon* Brand admits that once he restrained himself from murdering Corwin because Corwin was standing on his favorite rug. The rug in question is described, but unnamed; Zelazny notes, however, that it was a Kazak. Merlin has a Tabriz in his room in Castle Amber. In *Eye of Cat*, Yellowcloud tells Ironbear that before he will listen to him, Ironbear must "Roll up the rug first, though, and kick it out of the way. I'd hate to mess up a Two Gray Hills."[4]

Music

A nonvisual art form in which Zelazny has a serious amateur's interest is music. As with graphic arts, Zelazny does not limit his attention to one type of music, and his interest often is expressed in his writing. Although influenced by rock and roll in its earliest years, Zelazny's greatest fondness is for folk and jazz:

> I grew up in the Cleveland area where the term "rock 'n' roll" was coined by
> the dj Alan Freed. There came a point in the 50s where this sort of music
> poured almost constantly from the radio . . . I was not immune to the power-
> ful beat it possessed. It gave it a great feeling of immediacy, as well as one of
> physicality. Later developments, with heavy amps, feedback, & shouted lyrics,
> came to capitalize on the "event" nature of a performance – superseding the
> R&B roots which had come out of jazz . . . & I realized that its appeal, ulti-
> mately, was limited for me to a "wake-up" stimulation-effect . . . Folk & jazz
> were my first loves, though, nor have they faded for me. (letter, 7 July 1991)

Music has a unique relationship to the writing/composition process for Zelazny: "When I hit a difficult spot, I'll get up, put on a
record of the sort of music that hits the mood I want to create, and
maybe pace for an hour" (Sanders, 47). An example of this interrelationship between composition and music occurred when Zelazny
was writing "The Man Who Loved the Faoli." In the essay that introduces the story in *SF: Author's Choice 4* edited by Harry Harrison,
Zelazny discusses the difficulty he had coming up with a story to go
with the cover that Fred Pohl had sent to him:

> It was not until that evening while listening to the song, "We'll Sing in the
> Sunshine," that something clicked. It was the line, "But though I'll never love
> you, I'll stay with you one year" that did whatever was done. The graveyard
> world, the characters, the entire situation were suddenly all together – in
> short, the whole story. I sat down and wrote it in a matter of hours.[5]

Another story that was composed with musical assistance was the
novel *Doorways in the Sand*. Zelazny recalls that he listened to a
great deal of folk music, particularly the Clancy Boys album *The Rising of the Moon*, while working out precisely how the flashbacks
would work.

As it sets two of his enthusiasms, poetry and legend-lore, to
music, it is unsurprising that one of Zelazny's earliest musical interests was folk music: "I was a Kingston Trio fan in high school & college, as folk was one of my earliest musical loves, going back to Francis James Child's ENGLISH AND SCOTTISH POPULAR BALLADS and Bishop
Percy's RELIQUES OF ANCIENT ENGLISH POETRY" (letter, 8 January 1990).
While attending Columbia University for his masters degree, he took
advantage of his proximity to the Greenwich Village coffee houses
and clubs to expand his exposure to folk.

The influence of folk music on Zelazny's fiction is not limited to providing inspiration; it is also used to provide color. There are direct references or allusions to several pieces within stories. *A Dark Travelling* opens with a passing reference to the song "Eddystone Light." Other stories, especially those with characters with a contemporary Earth heritage such as the Ambers, allude to folk pieces.

In *Creatures of Light and Darkness* the section titled "Interlude in the House of Life" begins, "Osiris sits in the House of Life drinking the blood-red wine." This line is a direct play on the opening of Child's fifty-eighth ballad, "Sir Patrick Spens": "The king sits in Dumferling toune, / Drinking the blude-reid wine" (letter, 8 January 1990). The Steel General from the same novel, a cyborg rebel with a career centuries long, is a hero directly from a folk protest song. His humanity rests not in his flesh, which he replaces with metal as needed, but in his banjo on which he plays songs taught to him by Woody Guthrie.

Perhaps Zelazny's most extended use of folk music is in the novel *Changeling* and to a lesser extent its sequel, *Madwand*. Pol Detson, the protagonist, is a sorcerer's son, but when he is exchanged for a child of a more technological society there is no training to enable him to tap the wealth of power that is his familial inheritance. Alienated from his family and from the society in which he was raised by a peculiar personal aura that causes sensitive machinery to malfunction in his presence, Pol takes refuge in the music he makes on his acoustic guitar. The combination of his magical talent and his music permits him to weave intricate musical hallucinations. It also permits him to manipulate his environment in a fashion more controlled than the random glitches and accidents that prevented his working with machines. Folk music becomes the outlet for him to develop his powers, saving him from suicide after the fashion of Miniver Cheevy, the forlorn hero of Edward Arlington Robinson's poem of that title, with whom Pol feels such affinity that he sets the poem to music of his own composition.

Given Zelazny's fondness for both folk music and science fiction, it is to be expected that he is familiar with "filk," the peculiar hybrid musical form that has developed from the two. Filk takes the characters and themes of science fiction and fantasy and sets them to music, often to the tunes of folk standards. Although Zelazny does not compose filk, several of his stories have inspired filkers. Among

the strangest of these compositions are those by the band Hawkwind, whose style is more akin to hard rock than to folk. Hawkwind's
pieces include "Damnation Alley" and "Jack of Shadows."

Although Zelazny feels a great deal of affection for folk music, he
has used jazz more frequently in his writing. As with anything in
which he takes more than a passing interest, Zelazny has read extensively in the area and has a large library of tapes by a wide variety of
musicians. He regularly attends performances by the "Red Hot Chiles
Jazz Band," a Santa Fe group headed by his long-time friend Jere
Corlett, and as frequently as his schedule will permit travels to various jazz festivals.

Part of the fascination of jazz for Zelazny is its improvisational
character:

> That [improvisation] – as opposed to playing set pieces over & over, note for
> note the same each time – is what I like best about it; & this is what I think of
> rather than [particular] tunes, when I think of jazz. A good jazz band is a cre-
> ative machine, for on-the-spot creation, through which any interesting musical
> theme might be run, & I have no problem [with] the actual origin of the tunes
> themselves. (letter, 22 February 1990)

Therefore, some of the interest that jazz has for Zelazny may lie in
the fact that it does what he himself loves to do in his writing – improvise on what is familiar, whether that familiarity is a
myth, legend, form, or traditional approach to a topic.

Jazz pieces frequently receive cameos in Zelazny's stories, such
as the reference to Miles Davis's "Saeta" in the short story "A Thing
of Terrible Beauty." Often a title or a line quoted out of context is
mentioned in passing to add color to a scene. Zelazny often carefully
considers which piece to mention or which artist is appropriate to a
given setting. A fine example of the thought that goes into choosing
allusion can be seen in the Amber novel *Knight of Shadows*. Following a discussion between Random and Martin that clearly draws
on Zelazny's extensive knowledge of jazz trivia, the two play a rendi-
tion of "Wild Man Blues" on saxophone and drums. Zelazny comments on the scene:

> Martin being basically a rock musician – though Amber isn't electrified & he's
> using his sax – & Random being a jazz player, I had to find the right compro-
> mise. I didn't think Martin would try to get his dad to play rock (though he

might have been surprised if he had), but I didn't think he'd cave in & play early jazz. I figured that if he compromised it would be for post-Charlie Parker-type jazz – which is why I picked Richie Cole for the comparison I made. (letter, 30 September 1989)

Another detailed use of jazz occurs in the novel *The Mask of Loki*. Tom Gurden is a jazz pianist, a specialist in the form known as "stride." Stride is, to use Tom's own definition, "characterized on the left hand by an alternating bass note and chord – with the chord played one-and-a-half to two-and-a-half octaves higher than the note. The right hand meantime plays syncopated figures in thirds and sixths, chromatic runs, and tremolo octaves."[6]

Tom's fascination with jazz does not provide him with the uniform strength that Pol Detson's guitar playing does for him. Whereas Pol's playing gives him an outlet for feelings that he cannot express in any other fashion, Tom's music is an obsession that verges on monomania. Indeed, much of Tom's personality seems to be modeled on the self-destructive jazz musicians whose exploits have been distorted into legend. Tom cannot stay away from pianos, even after he learns that his life is in danger and that his enemies repeatedly track him through this addiction.

But Tom's fascination with jazz is a strength as well as a weakness. When he acquires the box in which the Knight Templars have kept the remnants of the Stone, his musical mind enables him to perceive each of the fragments as notes of music and thus deduce that the individual jewels are fragments of a larger whole. In the end, what Zelazny sees as jazz's greatest attraction, the power of improvisation and manipulation of patterns without losing the source, is the power that Tom draws on to merge the experiences of his many incarnations and finally defeat his enemies:

Tom Gurden knew things from the experience of his many lives that Thomas Amnet the Knight Templar could never have suspected. . . . Thomas Amnet had been a creature of Northern France. He had been a man of direct appetites and linear tastes. . . . His magic had been the brute force of fulcrum and lever: pull on it, and the truth sprang forth. But the complexities of jazz, the subtleties of a lysergic-acid high, the inverted physics of aikido – these would have been lost on the old crusader. (329)

Jazz and folk may be Zelazny's great musical loves, but his interest is broader than any single genre. Included in Oberon's funeral music in *The Courts of Chaos*, although never mentioned by name, is the "Ian Morrisson Reel" as played by Celtic harpist Alan Stivell (letter, 31 October 1989). In *Knight of Shadows* Merlin encounters the Pattern Ghost of his Aunt Deidre in a setting drawn directly from the World War II song "Lili Marlene"; in *Prince of Chaos* the Pattern Ghost of Corwin exits to strains of the same song played on the radio of Merlin's Polly Jackson Chevy. That same car radio allows Zelazny to introduce various musical allusions, supplying something like a soundtrack for the action alongside Corwin's Pattern. As Zelazny explains: the radio "always plays something appropriate for the mood and the action."[7] The songs that the car radio plays reflect not only the mood and action in *Prince of Chaos* but also the range of the author's tastes. Wynton Marsalis's "Caravan"[8] is jazz, while Renbourn's "Nine Maidens" is folk, but the references to "Sara K" (194) and "Bruce Dunlap" (144) are to New Mexican guitarists. Zelazny indulges in a bit of veiled self-reference when he mentions Dunlap's album *Los Animales*, as he wrote the liner notes for both this album and Dunlap's second album, *About Home*.

Martial Arts

Not all of Zelazny's enthusiasms are as nonparticipatory as his interests in art and music. He has studied various martial arts since college and continues to do so. One of the first martial arts Zelazny studied, and the only one that required a weapon, was fencing: "I'd taken fencing in lieu of regular Phys Ed, as I couldn't stand team sports. After the first year, the teacher had suggested I try out for the team and I did" ("Aikido Black," 7). Zelazny fenced for four years while in college, taking three varsity letters in the sport and captaining the epee squad in the final two years. He borrows this bit of personal history with little alteration for Godfrey Holmes, the protagonist of "This Moment of the Storm," who describes his own involvement with fencing as follows:

> I had not wanted to take General Physical Education, but four semesters of it were required. The only out was to take a class in a special sport. I picked fencing . . . I liked it. So I tried out for the team in my Sophomore year, made

it on the epee squad, and picked up three varsity letters, because I stuck with it through my Senior year.[9]

Fencing or more lethal sword-play occurs frequently in Zelazny's fiction. His personal experience influences the fashion in which he describes sword fights, allowing him to go into a professional level of detail. Yet, he is not simply repeating the jargon of an esoteric sport. When he is not dealing with merely human fencers, he alters the restrictions of the art to suit his setting: "All of the lengthier duelling sequences in the Amber books are properly choreographed for a rapier class weapon, rather on the heavy side, as the Amberites have the extra wrist strength to wield such a blade well" (letter, 24 February 1989).

Although Zelazny ceased actively fencing after graduating from Reserve, he still maintains an interest in the art, including studying some of the techniques belonging to non-European cultures. In *Prince of Chaos*, when Dalt battles the Pattern Ghost of Eric for possession of both Coral and the Jewel of Judgment, Merlin's commentary on the duel notes the alternating use of Japanese and European fencing techniques by the duelists, complete with a detailed vocabulary of technical terminology.

Zelazny's knowledge of and experience in unarmed combat is even more extensive than his understanding of fencing. In college he studied judo for two years, learning not only the sport but also purely combat related techniques from the teacher, who was a former Marine unarmed combat instructor. The course did not offer belt tests, so he was not ranked at that time. After Columbia, he studied judo again, stopping after being ranked as a green belt. While in the military, he studied karate briefly, again without being ranked.

For nearly the next two decades, Zelazny's involvement was passive interest rather than active participation, but in 1982 he began to study aikido, developing an enthusiasm that he retains to the present day. Aikido is usually termed a defensive art. Zelazny describes its evolution as follows:

Morihei Uyeshiba, the founder of Aikido, created the art by combining Daito-ryu Aikijutsu (a form of jujutsu) techniques [with] the footwork for the Shinkage (Shadow-sword) school of swordsmanship – i.e., in many of the techniques the attacking arm is captured in an Aikijutsu grip & then treated as if it

were a sword, the cutting movement then performed resulting in the execution of the throw. (letter, 6 August 1989)

Zelazny's teacher for nearly eight years was Phil Cleverly. Cleverly's influence on Zelazny went beyond instructing him in a martial
art into discussions about the parallels between the martial arts and
life. The various ways of responding to a physical threat in martial
arts mirrors the different ways people can choose to interact with
their own lives, even on the level of interpersonal relationships. In
"Aikido Black" Zelazny credits these discussions, interwoven as they
were with the examples of the aikido lessons, with helping him to
assess the manner in which he had chosen to interact with people
throughout his life. In the dedication of *Sign of Chaos*, "To Phil
Cleverly and our seasons in the sun: Thanks for all the *kokyu
nages*,"[10] the Japanese *kokyu nages* refers to full body throws and,
in the light of "Aikido Black," certainly refers to more than physical
technique.

The opening of "Aikido Black" seems chosen to illustrate their
relationship:

> In the only photo I have of Phil Cleverly he is throwing me to the ground with
> an effortless aikido technique which perfectly controlled my att--k. His shoul-
> der-length hair is unmussed, his *hakama* draped, almost artistically, over hip,
> thigh, leg. My feet are high in the air; his expressioı. is emotionless above his
> neat beard. The photo was taken by a passing photographer for the *New Mex-
> ican*, out early on a Saturday morning looking for human interest material.

Zelazny proved an apt pupil, eventually receiving his black belt.
When Cleverly moved to Albuquerque in 1988, Zelazny took over the
class:

> I enjoy aikido but I never wanted to teach it. However, my teacher . . . could
> no longer teach his Tuesday night class. I'd studied [with] him from white belt
> through black & he asked me to take the Tues. night classes, saying that
> teaching it is a very special learning experience. As I said, I didn't want to, but
> I've been doing it for about a year now & I realize that he was right. Also, I've
> come to enjoy it. Explaining something you know only at a reflex level does
> require a sort of intellectualization I'd never run those things through in the
> past. I discovered it to be almost identical to my earliest experiences in teach-
> ing at writing conferences & seminars. (letter, 21 March 1989)

Soon after his move to Albuquerque, Cleverly discovered that he had ALS (amyotrophic lateral sclerosis), commonly called Lou Gehrig's disease, from which he died in 1990.

In 1986, a conversation with Walter Jon Williams awakened an interest in finding an art Zelazny could practice without a partner. Cleverly suggested t'ai chi, and Zelazny signed up with Wasentha Young to learn the Yang style, short form. He stayed with her for two years, learning not only the form but also perfecting his knowledge of breathing patterns. Unlike aikido or judo, t'ai chi is an "internal" art. Zelazny, however, sees a relation between t'ai chi and aikido: "Both simple and subtle, t'ai chi shares with aikido a circular approach to controlling another's movements, unlike the tae kwon do (and later, the hsing-i) which is more direct and linear" ("Aikido Black," 10).

To better participate in the "attack" portion of his aikido lessons, Zelazny studied tae kwon do with Michael Robinson for seven months, starting in 1989. One of Zelazny's reasons for choosing Robinson as an instructor was because Robinson had also studied hapkido, a martial art related to aikido by way of aikijutsu but "much nastier." Although Robinson could not rank his students, Zelazny benefitted from the exposure to the other form. Zelazny stopped doing tae kwon do about a month after his yellow belt test, when he suffered a minor injury to the sole of his foot.

Another reason for Zelazny's not returning to tae kwon do after the foot injury healed was that he had learned of a new teacher, Rusty Hamilton, who taught hsing-i and pa-kua, arts that had long been on his "wish-list." Hsing-i and pa-kua are, like t'ai chi, internal arts, and Zelazny feels that his experience with each of these three forms enhances his ability in the others.

Unarmed combat techniques are frequently mentioned in Zelazny's works, enabling even his more cerebral protagonists to defend themselves. In several early stories, the characters use a variety of judo moves. The nameless protagonist of the *I Am Legion* stories uses judo in two of the three stories in which he is featured, both times with less than complete success. In "A Rose for Ecclesiastes" Gallinger uses a jujutsu move that he had worked out to defeat Ontro, the Fist of Malann. Conrad, the protagonist of *This Immortal*, both wrestles and boxes.

After Zelazny returned to active participation, the use of the material within his works became both more frequent and more detailed, reflecting the large body of knowledge that he had gained not only from his own experience but also from extensive reading in the area – at one point, he was reading as much as a book a month. As mentioned in the earlier section on jazz, Tom Gurden, the protagonist of *The Mask of Loki*, is a student of aikido, and his interest in this subtle defensive art, like his interest in jazz, is a metaphor for his less direct way of approaching threats.

In the short story "Mana from Heaven," the protagonist's girlfriend, Elaine, manages to get the upper hand in an apparently no-win situation by using her skills in karate, causing the bemused protagonist to reflect that he had forgotten that she was "second *kyu* in Kyokushinkai" (*Frost*, 174). In *Knight of Shadows*, Merlin uses an aikido technique to defeat the doppelgänger who assaults him on the Pattern. As with fencing techniques, Zelazny is not above using his expertise in the area to come up with a reasonable way to alter the move to fit the circumstances, and with aikido, in fact, such adaptations are fully within the structure of the form:

> And then my left hand fell upon the inside of his right elbow, in a maneuver a martial artist friend had taught me back in college – zenponage, I think he called it. I lowered my hips as I pressed downward. I turned my hips then, counterclockwise. His balance broke, and he fell toward my left. Only I could not permit that. If he landed on the Pattern proper, I'd a funny feeling he'd go off like a fireworks display. So I continued the drop for several more inches, shifted my hand to his shoulder, and pushed him, so that he fell back into the broken area.[11]

The story that best illustrates the wide variety of martial arts techniques Zelazny has incorporated into his fiction is "24 Views of Mount Fuji by Hokusai." Mari's skill in martial arts is not limited to her use of her *bo*, or staff. She also demonstrates her ability with more arcane, internal arts, most dramatically the one she uses to siphon energy from Boris during their love making. In "24 Views of Mount Fuji," the martial arts are more than devices used to beat off an attacker and then forgotten; they are woven into the theme and texture of the piece. The *goma*, or fire service, that Mari participates in demonstrates, according to the philosophy of the Japanese martial arts, how the same energies that can heal can also destroy; what matters is the knowledge and intent of the user. Mari's pilgrimage is not a sham meant only to fool Kit, but is her intense spiritual preparation for death. Even her final defeat of Kit is presented to him by her as *jigai*, the female equivalent of *seppuku*, or a suicide to restore honor. Without Zelazny's extensive knowledge of the martial arts as well as the cultures and attendant theories that both created them and evolved with them, "24 Views of Mount Fuji" would be a much more shallow story.

A final, more amusing side effect of the martial arts on Zelazny's writing is their part in influencing him to quit smoking, which between cigarettes and pipe he had done for 24 years. This decision may seem to have a limited connection to his writing, but according to Zelazny smoking had a distinct influence on his characterization:

> My characters smoked in most of my early stories because whenever I was momentarily stuck in the course of narrative I would light a cigarette. My usual reaction then was to transfer it. "Of course," I would think, "He lit a cigarette." (letter, 29 May 1989)

Even a quick survey of stories and novels following Zelazny's decision to quit smoking shows a marked drop in the number of characters who smoke. Apparently, when he broke the habit, this trick of characterization also vanished.

Places

Zelazny has always been a writer with a strong ability to invoke place, whether that place is real or complete fantasy. In the essay "Constructing a Science Fiction Novel," collected in *Frost and Fire*, Zelazny comments that setting is a special challenge for a writer of science fiction and fantasy, because setting is often what sets the material apart from mainstream fiction:

> Of the three basic elements of any fiction – plot, character, and setting – it is the setting that requires extra attention in science fiction and fantasy. Here, as nowhere else, one walks a tightrope between overexplaining and overassuming, between boring the reader with too many details and losing the reader by not providing enough. (*Frost*, 117-18)

To design settings for his stories, Zelazny often draws material from his own experience and adapts it to his need. The Ohio Francis Sandow recalls in *Isle of the Dead* is clearly the landscape of Zelazny's boyhood. Sometimes a striking landscape will contribute to the evolution of a story, as with "Permafrost," in which "the power of all that ice and cold" as viewed on an Alaskan cruise provided the germinating impulse for the story (*Frost*, 17).

Especially after his move to New Mexico, however, Zelazny began to set bits and pieces of his stories in the area around his new home, almost as if he was discovering new terrain and could not resist extending that exploration into his fiction. Some of these references are in passing, such as the New Mexico ghost town in that he sets "Unicorn Variation," the "southwestern state capital" which is the opening setting for *A Dark Travelling*, or Mari's mention that she is hiding Kendra in an isolated commune in the Southwest.

A particularly important part of Zelazny's southwestern landscape is the mountains, most particularly the Sangre de Christos range, of which he has an unobstructed view from the large window over his desk in his study. In the introductory note for "24 Views of Mount Fuji," Zelazny comments:

> I recall mentioning in a letter to my friend Carl Yoke something concerning the appearance of the mountains behind my home and having realized but recently that seeing them in a different aspect every season, every day – every time I look at them, actually – had a lot to do with the following story . . . Without my mountains there would have been no meditations, no story . . . Everything goes back to the mountains. (*Frost*, 201)

The same mountains, incidentally, provided the model for Mount Kolvir as drawn by Todd Cameron Hamilton on the title page of *The Visual Guide to Castle Amber*.

Zelazny's fondness for detail and accuracy comes out in how he uses the local landscape in his fiction. For the scene in *Bridge of Ashes* where Leishman shoots the governors of Colorado and Wyoming in downtown Santa Fe, Zelazny went down and walked through the area around La Fonda Hotel, making certain that Leishman could shoot the governors and then make his escape across the rooftops as described.

Several sequences in the Merlin Amber novels also take place in and around Santa Fe. Zelazny knew not only precisely which hotel

Merlin and Luke had rooms in but also which rooms were theirs and which table they sat at in the bar. When they leave the hotel to have dinner at La Tertulia, the route they take across parking lots and side streets is scrupulously accurate. In an example of place inspiring scene, Zelazny notes that the idea for the crucial scene where Luke and Merlin are ambushed on their way down from the Santa Fe ski basin came to him while making a similar drive and noticing how easy losing a body or bodies would be on that twisting road. Such attention to detail is particularly important in the Amber novels, where shadow-shifting can take a character from a recognizable reality into fantasy in the course of a short drive or walk. The fantasy sections benefit from being attached to such a concrete reality.

For the recent Wild Cards short story "The Long Sleep," Zelazny again returns to New Mexico for his setting. The majority of this story is set in the cities of Santa Fe and Los Alamos in the year 1952 – a time period for which Zelazny could not draw on his personal knowledge of the area. Zelazny places the action for the sections in Santa Fe largely in La Fonda Hotel, which has been around long enough to claim that Billy the Kid worked there as a dishwasher. The scenes set in Los Alamos were somewhat more difficult to do with accuracy, because the city had been closed to any outside traffic and extensive security checks were required to get in. Zelazny was determined to find what he could about the layout of Los Alamos, and his investigation included interviewing a woman who had lived there during the time in which he wanted to set his story.

A special case of place providing inspiration and setting for a story is the novel *Eye of Cat*. Whereas in the stories just noted Zelazny chose to use the setting for his piece, in *Eye of Cat* the setting itself became both the source of the story and one of the characters within it. Zelazny explains the integral relationship of setting to the evolution of *Eye of Cat* as follows:

> I have lived in the Southwest for nearly a decade now. At some point I became interested in Indians. I began attending lectures, visiting museums. I became acquainted with Indians. At first, my interest was governed only by the desire to know more than I did. Later, though, I began to feel that a story was taking shape at some lower level of my consciousness. I waited. I continued to acquire information and experience in the area. (*Frost*, 119-20)

After deciding on a Navajo for his protagonist – rather than the Hopi of his earliest outline – Zelazny developed a plot that centered around the question of "adapting," a trait for which the Navajos are renowned. In Billy Singer's case, he must learn to adapt to the modern world in which he feels increasingly alienated, even from his own people.

The settings of *Eye of Cat* represent the different aspects of Billy's dilemma. The cocktail party in Arlington, the visit to the home of his friend Yellowcloud, even the Interstellar Life Institute all represent the choices the more modern, technological world offers him. His traditional heritage is represented by the lands of the Navajo, Dinetah. To most readers, Dinetah is as alien as any far-off planet; here Zelazny added to his more usual research techniques the physical investigation of areas in which he wanted to set portions of the novel. As with the Amber novels, he sought to ground his fantastic material in a concrete foundation:

> Then, for purposes of achieving verisimilitude, I traveled through Canyon de Chelly with a Navajo guide. As I wrote the portions of the book set in the Canyon I had before me, along with my memories, a map, my photographs, and archaeological descriptions of the route Billy followed. This use of realism, I hoped, would help to achieve some balance against the impressionism and radical storytelling techniques I had employed elsewhere. (*Frost*, 123-24)

Zelazny's care resulted in a novel in which the land becomes a character in its own right, one which Billy believes communicates with him through the weather, the birds, and the animals. Even human artifacts, like the petroglyphs of the Anasazi, a people who vanished – perhaps owing to their inability to adapt – become a means by which the mute land reminds Billy of what he would be abandoning. Zelazny combines his physical depiction of Dinetah with the recounting of various Navajo legends that show why the land is more significant than merely the sum of rocks, shrubs, and sky. Thus, as the novel progresses, the reader is able to share Billy's sense of Dinetah as something more than mere real estate, but rather as a character who encompasses the wide variety of landmarks in which the heritage of the Navajos is inscribed. Without Zelazny's vivid depiction of Dinetah, the psychological battle that is the true theme of the novel would fail completely.

Zelazny's fascination with a number of the arts outside of writing has made his writing richer and more varied. A wealth of information, however, whether gained through books or through experience, is not enough to make a piece of fiction work. If the author cannot use that information creatively, the end product is not worth the reader's attention, no matter how much might be learned from reading it.

As mentioned earlier, Zelazny has done the majority of his writing in two forms, poetry and fiction. In the following three chapters, the focus will be on whether he has successfully used the wealth of information he has accumulated to create the written works on which his reputation rests.

Chapter Four

The Pervasive Influence of Poetry

Zelazny's Verse

Since almost the beginning of his writing career, Roger Zelazny has been noted for the poetic quality of his prose. In the often cited introduction to *Four for Tomorrow*, Theodore Sturgeon comments on Zelazny as a prose poet who does not fail to create believable plots and characters:

> Genuine prose-poets we have seen, but quite often they fail when the measures of pace and structure are applied. And we have certainly had truly great story-tellers, whose narrative architecture is solidly based, soundly built, and well braced clear to tower-tip; but more often than not, this is done completely with a homogenized, nuts-and-bolts kind of prose.[1]

Following Sturgeon's lead, critics and reviewers have either praised or condemned Zelazny's use of prose poetry according to their personal preferences. Despite this continued attention to the poetic style of Zelazny's prose, however, very little has been written about Zelazny the poet, the most extensive commentary being Ursula LeGuin's general introduction to Zelazny's second volume of poetry, *To Spin Is Miracle Cat*. Certainly, Zelazny's literary reputation is based on prose works, not poetry. Nevertheless, talent as a poet and interest in poetry have had a marked impact on his fiction. This shaping falls into two general categories: prose style and character development.

Before discussing the influence of poetry on Zelazny's works, it is useful to discuss how poetry affected his development as a writer. As has been mentioned, Zelazny's interest in writing as a profession crystallized early in his life. But the type of writing he wished to concentrate on was not as definite. Zelazny mixed writing poetry with prose throughout his formative writing years. In 1954, while still in high school, he published both the poems "Diet" and "The Darkness Is Harsh" and the short story "Mr. Fuller's Revolt" in *Eucuyo*, the school's literary magazine. Gradually, he shifted his writing focus more and more to poetry. By his own account, between 1956 and 1961 he wrote "nothing but poetry – incredible amounts of it, mostly bad, but improving somewhat as time went on."[2]

During this time Zelazny was also pursuing his master's degree in English Literature at Columbia University. As his major area of concentration was the Elizabethan dramatists, inevitably the tone, themes, and style of their works influenced Zelazny's own:

> In grad school at Columbia the power of the Elizabethans for me was immense. The birth and flowering of such great drama in such a short span represented for me a concentration of terrific creative forces, both poetic and in terms of the often romantic subject matter, causing me to return again and again to study these works. And the Tragedy of Blood was one theme having great appeal to a would-be poet. Lines and cadences from Marlowe, Kyd, Shakespeare, Webster, Tourneur, Marston – read and re-read aloud – still return to me at high moments in my own writing, roll about within my head, force feeble echoes. My fascination with the Faust theme, with bits of grotesque humor, with low counterpoint to high action, with Hamlet-like ironic commentary on action, with an occasional pun – all owe much to this period. I would be a very different sort of writer had it not been for early exposure to the "bloody Elizabethans." And at the time, what I wanted most to be was a poet. They are there, they are with me. (letter, 9 May 1991)

A pervasive influence on Zelazny's early poetry was Hart Crane, about whom he wrote the poem "Southern Cross (Elegy, Hart Crane)." In the foreword to *When Pussywillows Last in the Catyard Bloomed*, Zelazny says:

> Every generation seems to breed an eccentric, talented poet who dies young and becomes something of an idol to the next generation. Sylvia Plath was too late for me in this respect. In my day it was Hart Crane. I've read and still read a lot of poetry, but Crane's word magic probably had the most influence on whatever poetic style I may have. (2-3)

Other poets who influenced Zelazny's style include William Blake, A. E. Housman, W. B. Yeats, W. H. Auden, Dylan Thomas, and Robert Lowell. Like many novice poets, Zelazny developed his own style through pastiche, the imitation of the style of other poets. "Tryptych," written sometime between 1955 and 1960, borrows the voices and styles of Sappho, Li Po, and Rimbaud for three short, almost imagistic lyrics. The more irreverent Zelazny emerges in the poem "Decade Plus One of Roses," which won a poetry prize offered by *Skyline* magazine in April 1959. Taking the subject of roses, the poem parodies the styles of 10 modern poets ranging from Gertrude Stein through Wallace Stevens, tagging the beat poets on at the end. Through this parody Zelazny demonstrates both his familiarity with the modern canon and his own skill as a poet.

As Zelazny began to publish, many of his poems were well-received. In 1957 and again in 1958, he was awarded Western Reserve's Finley Foster Poetry Prize. At one point, he compiled a manuscript of his poems, gave it the title "Chisel in the Sky," and sent it to the Yale Younger Poets Competition – which it did not win. Eventually, he came to a decision about poetry as the basis for a writing career:

> In or about 1961 I realized that only Robert Frost and Carl Sandburg were making their livings writing poetry whereas numerous other authors were doing well under the wings of muses less comely. The writing was there on the washroom wall. I wanted to be a full-time professional writer. I made my decision and wrote the story "A Rose for Ecclesiastes" in October of 1961 and said good-bye to all that. (*Pussywillows*, 1)

Although Zelazny decided that writing poetry was not an effective means to make a living, he did not suddenly cease to be interested in the field. Through the present time, he continues to read poetry on a daily basis: "I read some poetry every day. It's the closest thing I can think of for a prose writer in the way of exercising the writing faculties as something like a daily run through a t'ai chi form might the body" (*Frost*, 12). Zelazny continues to follow the development of poetry. Favorites among contemporary poets include Diane Wakoski and W. S. Merwin. Merwin has earned Zelazny's peculiar praise for being a poet whose command of the language is so powerful that he can satisfy with image alone:

> But it wasn't really till I ran across W. S. Merwin's work that I realized I could be consistently happy with imagery alone when it proceeded from a person of extremely powerful vision and a personality that touched things with a tone I

found somehow congenial, reminding me again of someone else's observa-
tion: "The imaged Word, it is, that holds / Hushed willows anchored in its
glow." (*Frost*, 12)

Even though Zelazny largely stopped writing poetry in 1961 to
focus on prose, his poetry's influence on his prose remains so mani-
fest that examining his poetic style and themes in some detail is useful. The majority of Zelazny's published poetry is written in free
verse, although he occasionally employs more formal structures, as
in the aptly named "Sonnet, Anyone?"[3] He also employs placement,
writing poems structured by shape, such as "I Used to Think in Lines
that Were Irregular to the Right" or the diamond-shaped "Iceage."
Zelazny adapted what he learned from his studies in poetic structure
to the novel *Eye of Cat* in two ways. In the hard-cover editions of the
book the pages are printed with unjustified right-hand margins, because Zelazny thought "the rough-hewn, shaggy look of such pages
was [particularly] appropriate for mythic materials" (letter, 28
November 1989). This restructuring of traditional prose text form
was impossible to include in the paperback editions. In *Eye of Cat*,
Zelazny also uses poetic structures to help him gracefully break the
"show don't tell" rule of prose writing:

I captioned a section with each character's name, followed the name with a
comma and wrote one long, character-describing sentence, breaking its
various clauses and phrases into separate lines, so that it was strung out to
give the appearance of a Whitmanesque piece of poetry. . . . I wanted to make
this sufficiently interesting visually to pull the reader through what was,
actually, straight exposition. (*Frost*, 123)

Zelazny's poetry seems to have no favored length or structure.
The shortest of his published lyrics is one rich image describing
"Storm and Sunrise": ". . . machine of day pulling taffy" (*To Spin*,
41). Others, like "Riptide" and "Dreamscape" (*To Spin*, 33-34, 64-
65) run to more than 60 lines.

Caesura and enjambment are two of Zelazny's favored devices
whatever the structure of the poem. The poems "Dreamscape" and
"To Spin Is Miracle Cat," for example, were both written with complete punctuation, "which I subsequently removed as an experiment,
& thought . . . more effective [without] the obvious caesurae" (letter,

4 February 1991). Zelazny is also fond of word play, not only puns but more subtle homonymic relations, such as that between "peace" and "piece" or "heart" and "Hart" in "When Pussywillows Last in the Catyard Bloomed."

No matter the techniques that he uses to express them, Zelazny's themes are as varied as his structure and forms. Not surprisingly, some of these themes are similar to those that he often treats in his fiction. The poem "Thoughts of the Jupiterian Frantifier Fish" is science fiction in a free verse form influenced by the works of the Chinese poets Li Po and Tu Fu. The Faust legend, which colors stories like "For a Breath I Tarry" (the title of which itself is indebted to a line from A. E. Housman's volume of poetry *A Shropshire Lad*), appears in "Faust before Twelve." Mythology supplies images for many of his early poems, just as it did for his early stories. "The De-Synonymization of Winter" and "Awakenings" both draw on familiar Greek and Norse figures. "Brahman Trimurti" invokes Hindu deities. Still others, like "The Man without a Shadow," mingle Greek, Norse, and Egyptian figures with some of the disregard for strict mythological boundaries that Zelazny would later bring to *Lord of Light* and *Creatures of Light and Darkness*.

Many of his more prevalent themes, however, are ones that he chooses not to treat in his fiction; among these is the writing process as an act of creation. Many of the characters in Zelazny's novels and short stories are creators. The worldscaper Francis Sandow in *Isle of the Dead* can tailor planets to a client's specifications. The initiates of the Pattern of Amber can create new realities simply by imagining a place and then going to it. At best, however, these characters and their experiences provide metaphors for Zelazny's thoughts on writing as a form of creation. In the poems, Zelazny uses this intensive and highly structured form of writing to openly comment on the act of writing itself.

One of the things he discusses is the role of form in writing, an interest he is concerned with in fiction as well as poetry. "I Used to Think in Lines that Were Irregular to the Right," written in 1980, shows just how abiding Zelazny's concern with form remains:

> Prose is clean and smooth and slick,
> advancing fully to the right,
> building walls like rows of brick,

caging wild metaphors,
sealing their cells dead tight. (*Pussywillows*, 38)

Another poem that examines how form and structure can influence creative impulse is "Sonnet, Anyone?" "Sonnet, Anyone?" begins by asking the question "who wants the sonnet?" and then explains all the reasons why the sonnet is an unsatisfactory vehicle for the poet. The idea that the form of a poem is the "vehicle" through which the poet explores a thought is warped by Zelazny into an elaborate metaphoric pun:

> Save for Berryman's, who wants the sonnet?
> – A fusty hangover from ages dark.
> Take a thought, hang fourteen lines upon it,
> Prime it and crank it, force it to a spark,
> Then halting rhyme in pattern archaic,
> Play with the choke until the engine sings
> (Wondering when you'll get that certain kick),
> A stilted song of common imagings.
> While the oldfangled buggy, pushed with pride,
> Jolted to a motion, at times repays
> Mechanic hands, mostly it's a rough ride,
> With that Model T we drive on Sundays,
> Bumping down twisted country roads, my love,
> Where each must go who has something to prove. (*To Spin*, 18)

By the end of the sonnet, Zelazny has answered his own question. For him, at least, the sonnet is something he pursues to prove that he can write a sonnet, and so writes free verse from choice and not because he cannot write in more structured forms.

Structure is not the only aspect of writing that Zelazny discusses in verse. In many of the poems from the "More Recent" section of *To Spin Is Miracle Cat*, Zelazny addresses the uncontrollable nature of inspiration in his writing, a point he also discusses in the introduction to *Frost and Fire*:

> Science fiction is often referred to as a "literature of ideas." . . . Idea stories may go any which way, depending on who or what answers the Help Wanted ad. In fact, I occasionally have a strange (nonnegotiable) labor problem: The wrong characters will sometimes turn up and refuse to leave, staging a sit-down strike on the premises, i.e., the idea. I know they belong in another

story, and they're ruining the one they're trying to take over. Will they listen? No. It's like something out of Pirandello. (13)

For Zelazny, then, inspiration appears to be equal parts angel and devil, something he cannot do without, but also something that may attempt to take control of a piece. Two poems that perhaps provide the best illustration of this theme are "Locker Room" and "Riptide." "Locker Room" begins with a direct address from the writer to his words:

> You words damned well better do as you're told
> Get in line. Sound sweet. Stay on your feet.
> When I need a pun I'll ask for it.
> Match sound to sense, sense to sound. (*To Spin*, 15)

In "Locker Room" the problem of controlling inspiration is left unresolved. Despite a series of increasingly forceful (and crude, thus the poem's title) commands, the poem ends with the incomplete line: "Words can't walk out on"; the implied "me" and closing punctuation are both missing, using closure to illustrate that words can and will "walk out" on the writer.

In "Riptide" the discussion is longer and the theme more overtly stated: "The greatest argument I know for sadistic deities / is that inspiration comes in pieces / and some of them never fit" (*To Spin*, 33). Zelazny intersperses reflection on the unpredictability of inspiration, which may provide an image without a character or a character without a story, with samples of ideas that failed to develop into stories. Some of these, interestingly, have found their way into stories, since "Riptide" was written prior to 1981. "Itself Surprised" became the title of a story written for Fred Saberhagen's *Berserker Base* in 1984. The "Logrus" finally took shape as the antithesis and rival of the Pattern in the later Amber books, beginning with *The Trumps of Doom* in 1985. The majority of these ideas, however, many of which crowd two close-written pieces of paper tucked aside in Zelazny's study, will probably remain a mute testimony to the unpredictability of inspiration. As "Riptide" concludes:

> There may be things of which I shall never be free
> immortal as myself, bugging me down the ages,

proof against revenge
My world is crowded and an alien valley.
They sing against the closing of my eyes. (*To Spin*, 62-66)

Another theme that Zelazny deals with in his poetry, but rarely if ever in his prose, is his personal life. In other places, Zelazny has clearly stated that he draws a line between his fiction and his life: "I like to keep my writing apart from the rest of my life. I make my living displaying pieces of my soul in some distorted form or other. The rest of it is my own" (Sanders, xiv). For Zelazny the line between life and writing is less distinct when the writing in question is poetry rather than prose. In a discussion of the difference between the mindset in which he writes poetry as compared with that in which he writes prose, Zelazny explains:

> I realized that I have different feelings for the categories of poetry Aristotle describes as lyric – that being written in immediate relationship to the author – and dramatic – that done in mediate relationship between author & audience. I realized that for me the distinction between the "difficult" mindset of poetry & an "easier" one of prose is a measure of personal involvement, of closeness to my own psyche. (letter, 23 January 1991)

Therefore, part of what makes writing poetry a challenge for Zelazny is that it is a medium through which he can examine his own subjective responses to his environment. Perhaps the best of the poems written in this more personal vein is "When Pussywillows Last in the Catyard Bloomed." Zelazny recalls that he wrote it in New Mexico, "when in an unusually thoughtful mood" (letter, 4 April 1991). Like the poems that take the act of writing for their theme, "When Pussywillows Last in the Catyard Bloomed" begins with a reflection on a written line, but rapidly moves into more personal territory:

> When pussywillows last in the catyard bloomed . . .
> Fine line.
> Lacking an accompanying thought, perhaps,
> yet . . .
> My life is full of yets.
> We assemble ourselves slowly,
> collecting pieces (such as the above).
> Not all of them fit
> and some should not have

> but did (such as the above).
> Yet . . . I lack. Many things. (*Pussywillows*, 9)

The poem goes on to reflect on the many things the writer does have, as a consolation, perhaps, for the unnamed "many things" he still lacks. These things include simple temporal pleasures such as cats, constellations, and a pleasant yard from which to enjoy the world. This catalogue recalls "the simple, contemplative plea-sures – like good food, friendly cats, a pipe of pleasant tobacco – that make life worthwhile, despite all ugliness,"[4] that Zelazny once listed among the things he values. The poem goes beyond the comfort such things can offer, however, and confronts not only memories but also past and once possible selves. Here, paraphrasing Glendower in Shakespeare's *Henry IV, Part 1*, Zelazny summons the spirit of a possible self, from beyond:

> He was there. The me
> of me to come, memory-bound,
> unknowing, yet of yets,
> conjuring a self that did not come,
> as I call spirits from the vasty deep. (*Pussywillows*, 10)

If the speaker is the conjurer in his invocation of spirits, how-ever, he is more akin to Faust's summoned Mephistopheles in his analysis of his personal character. The line "I affirm what I affirm by denying / what I do not" recalls Mephistopheles' "I am the spirit which always denies" from Goethe's *Faust: Book 1*. In the end, having looked at past and present, the speaker moves on toward the future:

> I hang my yets on the catyard gate,
> booming where pussywillows
> last in the backward-turned time
> evolved their reply,
> whose accent denies my good-bye;
> Yet, yet and yet. And I walk
> singing not praise
> but wonder,
> part apart;
> imagined cats dance at my heels, at least as important, ever yet equally wise.
> (*Pussywillows*, 12)

In the final analysis, however, unlike a poet, a fiction writer must emphasize content and character over form, image, and structure. Sturgeon, despite his praise of Zelazny as one of the rare writers who can combine a prose-poetic style with both strong narrative and memorable characters, goes on to qualify his praise:

> One feels at times that a few (a very few, I hasten to add) of his more vivid turns of phrase would benefit by an application of Dulcote (an artists' material, a transparent spray which uniformly pulls down the brightness and gloss where applied). Not because they aren't beautiful – because most of them are, God knows – but because even so deft a wordsmith as Zelazny can forget from time to time that such a creation can keep a reader from his speedy progress from here to there. (*Four*, 9)

Certainly Zelazny has been fully guilty of letting his love for language overwhelm plot or character, for example in the legend and myth-littered text of *The Dream Master*, where the characters are weighted down with allusion and image. Nevertheless, these are stories and not poems, and the reader who is uninterested in delving into the subtext can still enjoy the story simply for the plot alone.

Further, Zelazny also differentiates between the prose poetry he may write in a story and poetry written for its own sake:

> the other day when we were talking about the hellrides in the Amber series, the scene in *A Dark Travelling* where the boy turns into a wolf, & places in *Eye of Cat* where prose & poetry seem to cooperate [with] each other, I realized on reflection that these sequences did not feel the same in their composition as any of the lyrics in my two books of poetry. . . . In these instances, I did go into something like that state of mind, but very quickly, & I wrote what needed to be written – again, very quickly – [without] the intensity of concentration which ordinarily accompanied the composition of poetry. It just "flowed." It occurs to me now that the fact that I did not think of it as the sort of poetry I write when I am writing "poetry" may have something to do [with] it. (letter, 24 January 1991)

Thus, Zelazny's prose poetry is a cultivated talent, evolved from the skills that he developed as a poet by deliberately combining the mindset of poetry with the texture of prose. Zelazny's ability to "flow" into poetic diction enhances the flavor of his science fiction and fantasy plots, allowing him to portray with greater realism the essence of environments that are outside of the strict bounds of what is most commonly defined as real. An example of this phenomenon occurs within the hellrides from the Amber novels. During a hellride an initiate of the Pattern in Amber can warp reality, effectively journeying from place to created place. To describe the phenomenon Zelazny most often resorts to prose poetry as is seen in this selection, drawn from Corwin's hellride in *The Courts of Chaos:*

> At my back, the sound of thunder, ceaseless . . . Fine lines, like the craqueleur of an old painting, abreast of us, advancing, everywhere . . . Cold, a fragrance-killing wind pursues . . .
> Lines . . . The cracks widen, blackness flows to fill . . . Dark streaks race by, up, down, back upon themselves . . . The settling of a net, the labors of a giant, invisible spider, world-trapping . . . (*Chronicles*, 2:340)

As this selection demonstrates, here Zelazny is using techniques more commonly found in poetry than in prose. In fact, the opening line "At my back, the sound of thunder, ceaseless," evokes Andrew Marvell's famous line from "To His Coy Mistress": "But at my back I always hear / Time's winged chariot hurrying near." As in poetry, sound and imagery are as important as strict definition. "Craqueleur" is chosen not only for its literal meaning but also for its onomatopoeic effect. The cold is defined as "fragrance killing," an image less precise and more exacting than any literal definition. The images of the net and giant spider both add a sense of menace that foreshadows the challenge from Brand, which will interrupt this portion of Corwin's ride.

Even the form Zelazny uses when describing the hellrides is similar to that of a poem. The short paragraphs substitute for stanzas; the ellipses create line breaks. Continuity is maintained through deliberately chosen images. In the passage selected above, the continuity between the first and second "stanzas" is achieved through the image of cracks and lines. The opening line of the next stanza, "Down, down and down," not only indicates the direction that Corwin finally chooses but also uses repetition to connect this passage to the one preceding it.

Another example of Zelazny's use of prose poetry to portray a less than normal situation occurs in *A Dark Travelling*. In this novel the protagonist, James Wiley, is an average 14-year-old with a hardly average family. His mother and sister are sorceresses, and he is a potential werewolf (like his Uncle George). When by accident he stumbles into an environment that triggers his latent lycanthropy, James finds himself shifting into wolf form, complete with a different range of senses and motivations. Zelazny gives this potentially clichéd situation an eerie beauty through his poetic description of James's altered perception of himself as "become a piece of the night": "I am suspended in the dark dream of the hunt, where reason sleeps as the scroll of sensation unwinds. I am dog-shaped death within the wood of the world, thing of fang and hunger. Beneath sky's eyes beast to feast blooding moon-turned hours."[5] The techniques in this passage are those more commonly found in poetry, not prose: alliteration, internal rhyme, metaphor, and image. Yet, the poetic language is not mere linguistic self-indulgence. Instead, it adds to the believability of James-as-werewolf, now perceiving the wood as a world and counting time by the moon rather than by clock.

The intricacies of language are not the only contribution that Zelazny brings to his prose from his background as a poet. The poet as a character type has occurred frequently in Zelazny's fiction. Zelazny comments in the foreword to *When Pussywillows Last in the Catyard Bloomed* that early in his fiction-writing career, when he was making the transition from poetry to fiction, poets and poetry kept appearing in his stories: "But poetry had a way of creeping into a few of those early stories – and when I needed a poem I still had batches of them to draw upon, though I'd chucked hundreds when I'd made my decision for prose. A few of those remaining fit stories here and there" (*Pussywillows*, 1-2).

One of the stories in which Zelazny uses both poetry and a poet protagonist is "A Rose For Ecclesiastes." Michael Gallinger not only is a poet; he defines himself almost as an extension of his art. When Morton, the commander of the expedition to Mars of which Gallinger is a member, summons Gallinger to his cabin he does not ask for him by name but rather calls him "that damned conceited rhymer" (*Four for Tomorrow*, 153). Gallinger lives up to Morton's assessment, refusing to associate with any member of the expedition except in the most general and abrasive fashion, preferring instead the company of his poetry and translations. Only after he has been humbled by his lover Braxa's rejection does he reassess himself, but even then he defines himself in terms of his calling. After M'Cwyie, the matriarch of the Martians, praises him as a holy man, a comparison he had not denied – had even invited – he responds: "I'm not a holy man . . . just a second-rate poet with a bad case of hubris" (190).

Another story collected in *Four for Tomorrow* that features a poet as a central character is "The Graveyard Heart." The poet Wayne Unger is already a member of the exclusive, near-immortal Party Set into which the protagonist, Alvin Moore, seeks and finally gains admittance. Unger is Moore's rival for the favor of the beautiful Leota Mason and is in many ways a far more interesting character than Moore. At one point, curious about his rival, Moore consults a bibliography of Unger's volumes of poetry. Among Unger's works is listed *Chisel in the Sky*, the title of Zelazny's own first, unpublished volume of poetry.

Whereas Moore actively desires both Leota and the Set, Unger has become cynical about both the woman and the society that shelters her. To him, the Set's immortality no longer seems like freedom from time but like freedom from experience, freedom from life. As a poet, Unger able articulates his dissatisfaction with both the time-ruled life of those outside the Set and the static, living death of the Set members through poems such as "Our Wintered Way through Evening, and Burning Bushes along It" and "In the Dogged House." Eventually, Moore finds himself unwillingly empathizing with Unger and using his poetry to give voice to his own discontent. Following his wedding to Leota, a wedding that along with her promise to return to the non-Set world has been his goal since the beginning of the story, he finds himself, much to his bride's dismay, quoting Unger's satirical "In the Dogged House," a criticism of the Set's Victorian moderator.

Despite this dissatisfaction and his reputation as a man of passion, however, Moore is not the one who strikes out against the Set; instead, the poet Unger acts by attempting to kill Leota. As Unger's somewhat disjointed attempt to explain himself to Moore shows, Unger sees Leota not only as a woman he has loved and lost but also as an extension of the Set who lures the living into immortal unlife: " 'Vampire,' he muttered, 'luring men aboard her Flying Dutchman to drain them across the years. . . . She is the future – a goddess on the outside and a thirsting vacuum within' " (*Four*, 104). Thus, in assaulting Leota, Unger is also assaulting the Set that has trapped him. Despite Unger's warning, when Moore learns that Leota will survive, he plans to wait for her. When the story ends, Moore lapses into the

cold sleep of suspended animation with the knowledge that he will
awaken in a world where "whatever else the new year brought, his
credit would be good" (113). Zelazny leaves for Unger the more difficult understanding that no matter how much he despises it, he will
never be free of the Set: "I'm suffering and I'll suffer more. There is
no Senta to save this Dutchman" (111). For Unger, as is emphasized
in his final conversation with Moore, the future is identical to his vision of Leota, a thing empty of promise and ultimately destructive.
Unger's only consolation is the dubious one of being able to articu-
late his misery in such a fashion that even the unwilling, like Moore
and Leota, can share his dark prophesy.

Another Zelazny poet protagonist is Corwin of Amber, the narrator of the first five of the *Chronicles of Amber*. When the story begins
in *Nine Princes in Amber* Corwin is suffering from amnesia, but even
before Corwin has walked the Pattern in Rebma and thus restored
his memory, he is able to remember that he is a poet and song
writer. As his brother Random shadow-shifts them back towards
Amber, Corwin's memory is stimulated for a moment by the sight of
the rich, purple-blue sea: "I found myself speaking in a language that
I hadn't realized I knew. I was reciting 'The Ballad of the Water
Crossers' " (54). Corwin eventually learns that this piece is the theme
of Amber's merchant navy and his own composition. Later, when
Moire, the ruler of Rebma, asks what he has done during his long absence from Amber, he tells her, "It occurs to me that I was a professional soldier, madam. I fought for whoever would pay me. Also, I
composed the words and music to many popular songs" (72). When
at last he walks the Pattern and his memory is restored, songs and
poetry are as integral to his personality as is the history through
which he has lived. One of the first memories he regains is "the voice
of Stephen Spender reciting 'Vienna' " (76). Another fragment is how
"I hummed a tune as we marched along and it caught on. It became
'Aupres de ma Blonde' " (76). As he remembers Amber, his diction
shifts from colloquial conversational to poetic: "I remember thy wide
promenades and the decks of flowers, golden and red. I recall the
sweetness of thy airs, and the temples, palaces, and pleasances thou
containest, contained, will always contain" (78).

Zelazny gives Corwin dimension beyond the usual sword and
sorcery hero by giving us hints of what depths of feeling Corwin is
capable. Much of this feeling is associated with poetry and song; in

fact, Corwin is given to reciting a quick line of poetry or bit from a song when moved. After Eric has Corwin blinded and tossed into the dungeons beneath Amber as penalty for his failed coup, it is not Corwin's strength or skill with a sword that saves him but rather the sympathetic poet who has co-existed within the warrior. The only person who dares to aid Corwin while he is imprisoned is Rein, minstrel to the Court of Amber. Corwin's friendship with Rein is based on a shared love for music and verse, a love that bridged the gap between the gifted prince and the gangling boy: "I wrote music, composed ballads, and he'd picked up a lute somewhere and had taught himself how to use it. Soon we were singing with voices together raised and like that" (133).

"The Ballad of the Water Crossers" is not the only piece of his poetry that Corwin recites in the course of the *Chronicles*. When he meets Ganelon, who had been his aide and then his betrayer long ago in a kingdom called Avalon, Ganelon asks him if he has heard of Avalon. In response, Corwin recites a short lyric that he claims to have heard from a passing bard, though he later identifies it as his own:

> Beyond the River of the Blessed, there we sat down, yea, we wept, when we remembered Avalon. Our swords were shattered in our hands and we hung our shields on the oak tree. The silver towers were fallen. How many miles to Avalon? None, I say, and all. The silver towers are fallen. (176)

The lyric evokes Avalon through a poetic image rather than through description, giving a sense of the sorrow Corwin feels for the enchanted land that is forever lost to him, though its shadows may continue to live in legend and Shadow. Given the personality of the narrator, his depictions of the quick, forced travel through Shadow so aptly called "hellrides" appropriately take on a rather eerie poetic beauty.

As has been noted in other sources, Zelazny did not write *Creatures of Light and Darkness* with the intention of publishing it. The fact that the book was written for his own "amusement" freed Zelazny from any restraints on his writing style. Therefore, the book is littered with poetry and poetic prose. Zelazny provides some basis for the inclusion of this poetry in the character of Vramin, the former Angel of the Seventh Station, who since the "title perished with the Station" (*Creatures*, 46) defines himself simply as a poet, although he is a competent magician as well. Vramin is an almost evangelical poet who uses his magic to "publish" his poetry: "He casts his poems at the nearest world, and wherever they fall they record themselves upon the hardiest substance handy. He boasts that he has written parables, sermons and poems in stones, leaves and brooks" (146). Two of Vramin's free-verse lyrics are included in full in the course of the novel, the untitled "Oh the moon comes like a genie . . . " which he recites as a backdrop to Horus's duel with the Prince Who Was a Thousand (138), and "Words," which is read but not comprehended by a band of the warriors of D'donori who encounter it "published" on a rock (145). A fragment of his poem "The Proud Fossil" is used to describe the archetypal city of Marachek-Karnak: "The sweetness of decay ne'er touched thy portals, for destiny is amber and sufficient" (105). The wording of this fragment is tantalizing apart from its descriptive purpose in *Creatures of Light and Darkness*, as it suggests a connection in Zelazny's mind between Marachek-Karnak and Amber, the immortal, prototypical city first described in *Nine Princes in Amber*, published the year after *Creatures of Light and Darkness*.

For Vramin, as his method of publication illustrates, there is a close link between poetry and madness. When at the story's end he departs to take up his new Station as the Angel of the House of Death, Horus wishes him "A fine poetry and a good madness," and Vramin responds, "Thank you, and I guess that's about all there is to be said" (190). Yet despite this seeming dismissal of any significance in Vramin's poetry, his poetry is given the final "lines" in the closet drama that ends the novel:

(Vramin raises his cane and a poem falls and blazes upon the floor.

Horus lowers his eyes to read it, and when he looks up again the green man is gone.

As the poem fades, the Angel of the House of Life knows that it was true but forgets the words, which is as it should be.) (190)

Zelazny does not give Vramin exclusive rights to poetry in *Creatures of Light and Darkness*. The narrative voice regularly lapses from prose to poetry. One of the first of these shifts is the long prose poetic passage that describes the "Awakening of the Red Witch." Later the identity of the Red Witch is revealed in the rhymed verse:

"Now, some say her name is Mercy and others say it's Lust. Her secret name is Isis. Her secret soul is dust" (63).

The narrative voice's greatest venture into verse, however, is the chapter "The Thing That Cries in the Night." This chapter is predominantly a long free verse narrative addressed by The Prince Who Was A Thousand to his wife, Nephytha. In this poem, the Prince traces history from the time that he ruled as Lord of Life and Death to the present day, when his struggle to find a way to destroy the Nameless has devastated everything that he had built, locking Nephytha herself into a bodiless existence as the genius of a watery world. As free verse lacks formal scansion and meter, it provides a medium that perfectly reflects the Prince's communication with his formless wife. He has saved her life by condemning her to a physical analog of free verse where she has only the form that he can give the "breath" of her life that remains after the Nameless' attack. The connection between Nephytha in her present form and poetry is accented when she says "I fear the madness that comes upon me" (67). Madness, as was noted when discussing the poet Vramin, is linked throughout *Creatures of Light and Darkness* to poetry.

At their first meeting, in the chapter "Place of Hearts Desire," Nephytha protests her existence as nothing more than "a breath, a color, a movement" (66). The Prince reminds her that she needs the form that he has given her to stay alive: "You require a place surrounded by water, to keep you alive. You require an entire world to keep you occupied" (67). Later, he explains to Nephytha that only after the Nameless is destroyed will he have enough power to re-embody her. She protests, "It is too much! It shall never be!" With her protest, the chapter shifts from free verse to prose, accenting her despair and foreshadowing her choice to die rather than continue to live as a breath of life trapped in an impossible world. Thus, by returning to prose for her protest and suicide, Zelazny chooses to have the structure of the text echo Nephytha's despairing desire to choose some other existence, even if it is the final form of death, over continuing as a bit of living free verse.

Another novel that incorporates poetry into the prose text is *Eye of Cat*. The protagonist of the novel, Billy Blackhorse Singer, is a Navajo Indian torn between the values of the twenty-second century in which he lives and those of the twentieth-century Navajo culture into which he was born. Complicating Billy's problem adapting to

the twenty-second century is the fact that he is alienated even from
the modern Navajos, who have changed over the two centuries since
his birth: "Paradoxically, then, he was on the one hand of an earlier
era than his contemporaries, and on the other . . . He had walked
beneath alien suns. . . . More traditional yet more alien he found
himself. He wanted to be alone, whatever he was" (20).

Additionally, Billy has trained as a shaman. As the surname
"Singer" implies, the Navajo shaman is taught poetry, the power
songs of his art. Billy is an extraordinary representative of this profession, because he not only uses and adapts the traditional songs
but is a poet himself and writes his own songs. Billy's songs are one
of the ways that he bridges the gap between the worlds in which he
lives. An example of this is Billy's song about travelling through the
trip boxes. On the twenty-second century Earth in which Billy lives,
nearly all travel is done by means of a network of conveniently
placed boxes (somewhat like the stepping discs that Larry Niven uses
in his Known Space universe). The traveller enters a box, gives his or
her destination coordinates, and then inserts a credit slip. Travel between points is nearly instantaneous and to most of Billy's contemporaries hardly worthy of notice. Billy, from his position between
times and cultures, wonders at what happens when he travels in this
fashion and composes a song to comment on it:

> Traveling the distance from hill to hill,
> passing from place to place as the wind passes,
> trackless. There should be a song for it,
> but I have never learned the words.
> So I sing this one of my own making:
> I am become a rainbow, beginning there
> and ending here. I leave no mark
> upon the land between as I arc
> from there to here. May I go in beauty.
> May it lie before, behind, above and below,
> to the right and the left of me.
> I pass cleanly through the gates of the sky. (38)

As the content makes obvious, despite the chanting rhythm and
meter of this poem, the poem originates with Zelazny. In fact, all of
the poems in *Eye of Cat* are in Zelazny's own language. In many
cases, he paraphrases actual Navajo material, much of which he
drew from Mary Wheelwright's 1956 book the *Great Star Chant and*

the Myth of the Coyote Chant. In other cases, Zelazny infuses Navajo
material with material from other American Indian cultures, thus reflecting both the adaptability of the Navajo and Billy's own familiarity
with anthropology. Billy's farewell to the lands of the Navajo when
he departs to meet Cat (58-59) is a good example of this fusion, as is
the poem that follows Ironbear's decision to pursue Cat and Billy.
This latter poem which draws its imagery from the Ghost Dance used
in American Indian religion, a religion that itself blended the traditions of many American Indian cultures, is appropriately placed, as
James MacKenzie Ironbear is not a Navajo; he is half-Oglala Sioux
and half-Scot. For him, however, Billy Singer, like the Ghost Dance,
transcends a specific American Indian culture. Ironbear wants to
help Billy "because he's an old-style Indian, and because my father
might have been that way. At least I think of him that way" (167).

Although, as mentioned above, Zelazny finds that writing poetry
and writing prose take radically different mindsets, so much so that
he rarely writes poetry when writing prose, he found that the poetry
for *Eye of Cat* developed fairly easily. He credits this to the fact that
the poetry was an extension of how Billy thinks and so developed
from the character. Interestingly, there was a reciprocal relationship.
The ghost train from *Eye of Cat* found its way into Zelazny's poem
"Dreamscape," which was written at approximately the same time as
Eye of Cat. In the latter portion of *Eye of Cat*, Billy returns to the
canyons of Arizona in a final attempt to evade Cat. There he has a vision of Smohalla's ghost train bearing on it all of his dead, including
his wife, Dora, for whose accidental death he still blames himself. An
almost familiar figure, who may very well be the recently slain Cat,
boards the train. In "Dreamscape" the same ghost train cuts through
a quiet "two-piano" Sunday afternoon, which is as haunted in its
own way as Billy's canyons: "The notes have reached the dancer / at
the center of the earth . . . / The train bearing dead relatives / will
come . . . " (*To Spin*, 64). Zelazny's use of this image differs greatly
between the novel and the poem. In *Eye of Cat* the ghost train has a
peculiar appropriateness. When the train approaches, Billy thinks:
"A train such as he has not beheld in years is coming. Coming impos-
sibly through this impossible place" (183). In "Dreamscape" the
train is the intrusion of the unreal and of death into the ordinary
world, blocking out the ordinary and forcing contemplation on the
dream:

> The train fills
> throb and eyes
> like coded bullets . . .
> I cannot see
> the mountaintop. The
> shadow grows before
> the engine. The world
> belongs
> to the dancer, the dance
> belongs
> to the dream.
> *Dead eyes and iron thrust.* (*To Spin*, 65)

Although Zelazny gave up poetry for prose more than three decades ago, his experience with and love for poetry continues to shape his prose in content, style, and character. Interestingly, the intertwining of these disciplines has become so thorough that, as in "Dreamscape," his prose now colors his poetry.

Chapter Five

The Zelazny Hero?

Critical Approaches

Critics writing about Zelazny's characters often labor under the mis-
apprehension that his protagonists fit neatly into one cleverly designed category. This tendency to stereotype his protagonists has
been used to praise, censure, or summarize his writing depending on
the interests of the writer. Nor are all of these categories identical, as
one would expect if the Zelazny protagonist truly conformed to a
certain mold. In his *Trillion Year Spree*, Brian Aldiss comments that
Conrad, the protagonist of *This Immortal*, is "one of many such in
Zelazny's work – a man skilled in the martial arts, blessed with cun-
ning, insight, and a poetic tongue."[1] Protagonists from novels
spanning Zelazny's career – such as Conrad from *This Immortal*
(1966), Corwin from the Amber books (1969-78), and Billy Blackhorse Singer from *Eye of Cat* (1982) – do fit this definition, but they
are hardly restricted to this type, as Aldiss implies.

Another restrictive categorization of Zelazny's protagonists,
clearly meant as praise, occurs in Joseph V. Francavilla's article
"Promethean Bound: Heroes and Gods in Roger Zelazny's Science
Fiction." Francavilla opens his article with the sweeping statement:

> Despite the apparent differences between heroes in Roger Zelazny's science
> fiction, such as Mahasamatman in *Lord of Light*, Conrad Nomikos in *This
> Immortal*, and Francis Sandow in *Isle of the Dead*, they all conform to a par-
> ticular model. With amazing virtuosity, Zelazny has used this model and has
> produced story after intriguing story, with fresh variation in locale, religious
> framework, and mythological background.[2]

Francavilla goes on to discuss a hero who is indebted to the myth of
the Fisher King as presented by Sir James Frazer and Jessie Weston,

the mythological hero as described by Joseph Campbell in *The Hero with a Thousand Faces*, and, as the article title suggests, the myth of Prometheus, both as reported in classical mythology and as used by Percy Bysshe Shelley in *Prometheus Unbound*. Francavilla supports his thesis with analysis of only the three novels mentioned above and passing references to three short stories. Although the article was published in 1985, none of the texts on which Francavilla bases his analysis are more current than 1969. Moreover, the archetypes that Francavilla compiles to construct his all-encompassing Zelazny protagonist are varied and contradictory enough to cover almost any thesis.

Another critic who attempts to unite all the Zelazny protagonists into one category is Theodore Krulik, author of the 1986 study *Roger Zelazny*. Krulik begins his preface by stating that "In pursuing my research for this book, I found it virtually impossible to separate the man from his writing" (ix). Not surprisingly then, Krulik's analysis of the Zelazny protagonist relies heavily on his personal perception of Zelazny. Krulik states:

> In breathing life into his characters, he has developed a particular type of protagonist. Typically, he is tall, cultured, highly perceptive and intelligent, artistically or creatively talented, who bears up in spite of some deep personal loss, and who reveals his inmost feelings and secret thoughts to the reader. This singular character persists through many of Zelazny's works, from Michael Gallinger . . . in "A Rose for Ecclesiastes" to William Blackhorse Singer in *Eye of Cat*. In these and other protagonists, the reader glimpses the face of Roger Zelazny. (7)

Once again, although the category is broad enough to permit quite a range of characterization, it cannot cover all of Zelazny's protagonists. Hell Tanner from *Damnation Alley* is not at all cultured. Jack from *Jack of Shadows* may be cultured, but he is hardly sensitive. Dennis Guise in *Bridge of Ashes* may have the knowledge of many intelligent men, but he is unable to put that knowledge to any productive use.

The critical assessments quoted above are not a complete catalogue of critical attempts to deal with the range of Zelazny's protagonists by categorizing them; rather they are meant to serve as a representative sampling of current criticism. Investigation of the whole of Zelazny's canon shows that Zelazny's protagonists cannot be neatly put into one category. There are types that certain characters fit, but even these are not interchangeable, even to the extent that, for example, many of Heinlein's crotchety sages can be interchanged. Zelazny discusses his interest in variations on certain types in the introduction to his short story collection *Unicorn Variations*:

> Gore Vidal has suggested that a writer has a limited cast of characters – his own repertory company so to speak – and that, with different makeup, they enact all of his tales. I feel he has a point there, and that this constitutes yet another limitation (though I like to feel that over the years one can pension off a few, and I do try to seek out new talent).
>
> All of these things considered, it is not surprising that one can detect echoes, correspondences and even an eternal return or two within the work of a single author.[3]

One thing that Zelazny does insist on for his protagonists is that however they begin the story they have changed by the end:

> I think that the rhythms of a story, whatever the details of the narrative, require that the protagonists be changed in some fashion by the action. It's not enough just to put them through the paces. They have to be different at the end than they were at the beginning.
>
> (Okay. This excludes morality play allegorical figures, humor-dominated characters in a Jonsonian play & Grimm's fairy tale figures. But these are specialized forms of narrative, too. I'm talking general short stories & novels.)
> (letter, 8 February 1990)

As Zelazny has developed as a writer, the range of his characterization has also developed. Among others, Fred Cassidy from *Doorways in the Sand* (1976), James Wiley from *A Dark Travelling* (1987), and Merlin, son of Corwin from the latter Amber books (1985-91), challenge the commonly held notion that the Zelazny protagonist is always an almost too competent, heroic, semi-immortal. Perhaps the protagonist who most clearly demonstrates Zelazny's continual efforts to broaden his range is Mari, the heroine of the 1986 Hugo-winning story "24 Views of Mount Fuji by Hokusai."

An in-depth study of the Zelazny protagonist is best pursued in two distinct parts. First, it is interesting to discuss at some length the themes and traits to which Zelazny repeatedly returns. Second, it is imperative to examine the use of heroic and less than heroic figures in the course of Zelazny's writings. Although it would be tempting to try to address these questions in every novel and short story, with 30-plus novels and countless short stories, the task would be unmanageable, even in a book-length study.

Themes and Traits

One of the most commonly recurring traits for a Zelazny protagonist is immortality. Zelazny credits the trilogy by George Sylvester Viereck and Paul Elderidge, *My First Two Thousand Years: The Autobiography of the Wandering Jew*, *Salome: My First Two Thousand Years of Love*, and *The Invincible Adam*, with influencing his interest in immortal characters in fiction. These novels deal with the adventures of the Wandering Jew, Salome, and a curious proto-man named Kotikokura. Zelazny says: "When I was growing up I read the 2000-Year Trilogy (each volume told from a different viewpoint) many times, & was doubtless influenced thereby in my own writing" (letter, 29 August 1990). Zelazny's interest in immortals is marked. Well over half the protagonists in his novels are either immortals or achieve some form of immortality.

To successfully investigate the way Zelazny's use of immortality shapes his protagonists, the term *immortality* as he uses it must first be defined. A Zelazny immortal is not unable to die. He or she has, however, usually found a way to avoid aging and illness, the most usual, nonviolent causes of death. The Zelazny immortal, however, can die as a result of violence, as is demonstrated by the deaths of several of the members of the royal family of Amber.

An excellent article on immortal characters in Zelazny is Joseph Francavilla's "These Immortals: An Alternative View of Immortality in Roger Zelazny's Science Fiction." Francavilla examines the tradition of immortals in fiction and notes that:

> Zelazny departs from the traditional dystopian view, and he presents these heroes as not bored, but curious, not isolated from the living, but in their midst, and not stagnant, but changing and maturing. These heroes are vital, active, demigods, neither incorporeal, wretched, nor apathetic.[4]

Even those immortals, such as Billy Blackhorse Singer of *Eye of Cat*, who do grow weary of their long lives can be encouraged to become actively involved in their worlds again as Billy is enlivened by Cat's challenge. Since Zelazny takes the view that immortality provides expanded opportunity for growth and knowledge, there is no wonder that the immortal has become such a pervasive character type for him; simply stated, immortality permits more complex characters.

Some characters are born into immortality, such as Conrad of *This Immortal* or the scions of Amber. Others acquire it through technology, as did Francis Sandow of *Isle of the Dead* or the major characters in *Lord of Light*. Sometimes immortality takes peculiar shapes. Jack of *Jack of Shadows* has a certain number of lives to exhaust. The Family in *Today We Choose Faces* shares a serial immortality, where personal identity passes without loss of memory from mortal nexus to the next mortal nexus. Red Dorakeen and other of the dragons of Bel'kwinith age in reverse, eventually trading their juvenile human form for the mature dragon form. So, although Zelazny's fascination with immortality has not waned, his attention to variation on the theme has kept his characters from becoming clichéd.

Not surprisingly, given the recurring use of immortals, many of Zelazny's protagonists are often associated with some legend or myth. Sometimes these legends belong to existing lore. In other cases, Zelazny creates the legend for the character. Some of the existing legends that Zelazny has drawn on are Greek (*This Immortal*), Hindu/Buddhist (*Lord of Light*), and Navajo (*Eye of Cat*). One of the most complex systems of allusions to legend occurs in the Amber books, where allusions to myriad legends and myths support the contention that Amber is the reality from which all other realities take their forms.[5]

Other characters belong to legends and myths created by Zelazny for his own use. *Isle of the Dead* and *To Die in Italbar* both use the Pei'an mythology with its complex pantheon of deities that incarnate through mortal symbiots. Jack of Shadows is a figure out of legend in both the light and darkside worlds wherein he dwells. Dilvish, the protagonist of *Dilvish the Damned* and *The Changing Land*, returns from Hell after a considerable period of time to find that he has become a legendary hero.

Yet despite Zelazny's fondness for myths and legends, his characters do not merely mimic the figures whose names or histories they bear. Conrad in *This Immortal* uses the legends associated with him, but rarely permits the legends to dictate his actions. He may be a hero to others, but he himself does not believe in heroes: "A man named Thomas Carlyle once wrote of heroes and hero-worship. He too was a fool. He believed there were such creatures. Heroism is only a matter of circumstances and expediency" (101). For *Lord of Light* Zelazny does not attempt to give authentic portraits of the Hindu deities whose names are used in the novel, since the novel is about mortals playing at being gods, not about those gods reincarnated as mortals. In fact, the theme of the novel could be that mortals, no matter how technologically sophisticated, cannot be gods without learning more than simply how to keep from dying.

The protagonist's desire to establish self-identity despite association with a legend or myth is even stronger in those books where Zelazny has created the legend. Francis Sandow in *Isle of the Dead* resists acknowledging that Shimbo, Lord of Darktree Tower, has a separate identity from his own, preferring instead to believe that the Pei'an god is a psychological projection, taught to him by his Pei'an mentor as an aid in terraforming. When Dilvish the Damned returns from Hell, he is quite uninterested in his own legend and, instead of resting on his earned notoriety, sets out on a vendetta against the wizard who had banished him to Hell.

An interesting variation on the motif of protagonist-become-legend occurs in the short story "The Keys to December," in which the protagonist, Jarry Dark, after his beloved's death, works counter to the plans of the Coldworld Catforms in order to preserve the alien Redforms. Jarry, does not feel that his motives are purely altruistic, however. He explains:

> I am their god. My form is to be found in their every camp. I am the Slayer of Bears from the Desert of the Dead. They have told my story for two and a half centuries, and I have been changed by it. I am powerful and wise and good, so far as they are concerned. (*Doors/Lamps*, 70-71)

Jarry is changed by the responsibility of his deification by the Redforms. Unlike those of Zelazny's protagonists who try to deny their associations with legends, Jarry courts his. Oddly, therefore, although he will die sooner than those of the Catforms who remain in suspended animation, Jarry achieves an immortality greater than that attainable through mere science. In fact, Jarry has learned what the deicrats in *Lord of Light* failed to learn – and what Sam apparently suspected – that the personal self must die before one can become absorbed into legend and achieve true immortality.

There is one legend that Zelazny is particularly fascinated by, enough so that he has incorporated it into several of his protagonists and used it as the underlying structure for his second collaborative novel with Robert Sheckley. This legend is that of Faust. Zelazny is familiar with the legend in its many forms, including the dramas of Christopher Marlowe and Goethe, both of whose texts he specifically alludes to in both poetry and prose. One of these deliberate Faustian allusions occurs in *Eye of Cat* when Billy is meditating over his pact with Cat. Zelazny commented how his admiration for Marlowe's *Doctor Faustus* shaped the language in this portion of the novel:

> so much fine language there, "See, see where Christ's blood streams in the firmament!" which I just had to echo in the 8th paragraph of EYE OF CAT, to indicate the Devil's Pact nature of Billy's deal [with] Cat – "He looks to the skies, but Christ's blood does not stream in the firmament." (letter, 29 August 1990)

As with other existing legends that he has incorporated into his fiction, however, Zelazny adapted and reshaped the Faust story for his own purposes. Perhaps the most obvious allusion to the legend, outside of *If at Faust You Don't Succeed*, occurs in the novella "For a Breath I Tarry." Allusion may be too subtle a term, since "For a Breath I Tarry" is essentially a retelling of the Faust legend with an ending more in Goethe's tradition than in Marlowe's. The Faust of Zelazny's tale is a sentient computer euphoniously named Frost. Frost is not torn between service to God and the Devil, but between Solcom and Divcom, two master computers built to tend and rebuild a postholocaust earth. At the story's opening, these entities discuss Faust in a dialogue strongly reminiscent of the "Prologue" of Goethe's *Faust: Part I*. As Faust had his Mephistopheles, so Frost has Mordel, a computer that assists him as he tries to understand what it was to be human. After numerous experiments with other ways of understanding humans, Frost manages, despite the objections of Solcom, to have his sentience transplanted into a blank-brained human clone. Thus, the choice Frost makes is the Faustian choice to pursue knowledge over slavish obedience to a higher power. Frost's pursuit of knowledge of humanity is rewarded in a somewhat ironic fashion when Frost finds that being human frightens him because of its imprecision, the very thing that a knowledge-hungry Faust seeks to avoid. Yet in the end, Frost not only resigns himself to being human, he accepts and welcomes it, inviting Beta, his counterpart computer, to become a human woman and share his life with him.

Although no other of Zelazny's protagonists is so overtly Faustian, many make bargains that invoke the Faustian extremes of knowledge or damnation. Charles Render, the "dream master" of the novel of that title, is tempted into a partnership with Eileen Shallot based on his pride in his ability as a therapist. Unlike Frost, he fails to dominate his "devil" and is damned to a mad eternity as Tristam to Eileen's Isolde. In *Lord of Light* Sam refuses the conventionally Faustian temptations offered to him by the rakasha (demons) of Hellwell, but wants to strike his own bargain for some military aid. The demon ends up finding himself in the uncomfortable position of learning more than he wished from his association with his Faust. After he learns to experience guilt from Sam, Taraka says: "Men suffer when they break pacts with demons . . . but no Rakasha has ever suffered so before."[6] *Damnation Alley* contains something of an inverted look at the usual Faustian pact, for Hell Tanner, whose name places him with the devils rather than with Faust, is given his freedom in return for agreeing to deliver medication through the aptly named Damnation Alley. Another interesting pact relationship is that between Dilvish the Damned and his mount, the Black. Although Dilvish met the Black in Hell and apparently made some agreement with him, an agreement that Dilvish, at least, believes to be Faustian, the Black's involvement may be quite differently motivated. At the end of *The Changing Land*, the Black produces the pact between Dilvish and himself and destroys it. Surprised, Dilvish says: "You meet the damndest people in Hell . . . I sometimes doubt you really are a demon," to which the Black replies, "I never said that I was."[7] In fact, despite his apparently hellish origin and fondness for a drink he calls "demonjuice," little indicates that the Black is a demon. He is a loyal companion to Dilvish, faithful to the spirit rather than the letter of whatever agreement they have made.

Heroic Protagonists

Zelazny's long-time familiarity with the heroes of myth and legend means that when he does create a heroic protagonist in his fiction those protagonists show the influence of their mythical forbears. The two best illustrations of this heroic protagonist in Zelazny's novels are Francis Sandow from *Isle of the Dead* and Billy Blackhorse Singer from *Eye of Cat*.

Francis Sandow and Billy Singer both have appropriately heroic pedigrees. Many classical heroes are of divine or semidivine parentage. As mentioned above, Sandow is a divinity, although not a human one. Instead, he has taken on the identity of the Pei'an god, Shimbo of Darktree, Shrugger of Thunders. When the story begins, Sandow has come to terms with this divine symbiosis by explaining it as a part of his training as a worldscaper: "One has to be able to feel like a god to act like one" (129). By the end of the novel, Sandow realizes that Shimbo has an independent identity – an unsettling realization for a rather strong-willed human. In *Eye of Cat*, Billy is not a divinity, but rather sees himself the chosen of his god: "he saw that Blackgod, who had chosen him, had kept his promise, making him into the mightiest hunter of his time" (56). This patronage overshadows his entire life, guiding his choices. When Billy fights his last battle, he has a vision of his gods joining him to fight his enemy.

Enhancing Sandow and Billy's divine heritages and setting them apart from the people of their own times is their technologically expanded life span. Sandow adjusts to the discovery that he is "possibly the oldest man alive, doubtless the only survivor of the twentieth century" (74) by panicking and then turning to the alien Pei'an for guidance. Billy Singer also adjusts to similar circumstances by associating with aliens, but the majority of his aliens are nonsentient animals that he tracks and captures for the Interstellar Life Institute. For both Sandow and Billy, age and attendant experience relative to the others of their race make them aliens among their own people so that, ironically, they feel less out of place among those creatures that are truly different.

Although many nonheroic characters have quests, it is rare to find a true hero who is not actively in pursuit of some goal. What is most interesting about the quests that both Sandow and Billy Singer undertake is that the quests force these heroes out of retirement and reluctantly into activity. Sandow is one of the hundred wealthiest men in the galaxy, and so little exists that can tempt him from his chosen solitude. When the Pei'an Gringrin-tharl sets out his lure for Sandow, however, Sandow not only takes the bait, he does so with a sense that the life of the secluded rich is not what he wants: "I watched the spinning stars, grateful, sad and proud, as only a man who has outlived his destiny and realized that he might yet forge himself another, can be" (29-30).

Billy Singer, while not wealthy, also believes that he has achieved all that is left for him: "It seemed too much of an effort for an individual to adapt any further. . . . Perhaps it was right to walk away from it now in beauty and die like the legend he had become" (56). Yet when the government woos him as the one man who can defeat an alien assassin, his curiosity and pride are awakened. To succeed in this task, Billy enlists the alien hunter, Cat, whose fee is Billy's life. The full awakening occurs when Billy learns that what Cat wants is not only Billy's death but an opportunity to hunt Billy, just as long ago Billy had hunted Cat. Suddenly, Billy values the life he had been willing to discard only days before: "Let it be very close and clean, he felt. Or else what the joy in such a context? This was the most alive he had felt himself in years" (95).

Another fascinating element shared by the quests of Francis Sandow and Billy Singer is that in both cases the initial quest and the initial enemy prove to be merely preludes to the confrontation of something much more psychologically complex. Sandow's initial goal is fairly direct. To free the people that Gringrin holds prisoner, Sandow must take Gringrin's challenge and meet the Pei'an on the alien's chosen ground. Yet when Sandow arrives on Illyria, he quickly learns that Gringrin is no longer his chief enemy. Gringrin has been defeated by one of his prisoners, a ruthless man named Michael Shandon, who had died trying to murder Sandow. Just as Sandow is also Shimbo of Darktree, so Shandon bears the name of Belion, Shimbo's traditional enemy.

Although Sandow quickly adjusts to the idea that Shandon rather than Gringrin is now his enemy, he is slower to adjust to the idea that Belion is also a factor. He is forced to face this when, having reached an accord with Shandon, Belion and Shimbo make themselves known: "Ours had been a series of subsidiary conflicts, their resolution unimportant to those who controlled us now. . . . So we stood there regarding one another, two enemies who had been manipulated by two older enemies" (168-69). When the battle between Shimbo and Belion is over, Shandon is dead, as are all but one of the people who Sandow had come to rescue. Yet the quest has not been a failure. Sandow may not have achieved his immediate goal, but he has learned to accept the truth about his relationship with Shimbo. His final actions and reflections before leaving Illyria make clear that despite his angry rejection of Shimbo when the god usurped his body, he will call on Shimbo again; although he now must acknowledge that Shimbo is more than a mere "psychological construct," he will continue to call upon the powers of the god for creation.

Billy Singer's quest is also multilayered. As mentioned above, Billy's initial challenge is to stop an alien assassin. His second challenge is set for him by Cat: "My full revenge requires the joy of the hunt. So I will make you an offer . . . Let us call it a week. Keep alive for that long and I will renounce my claim upon your life" (89-90). Through a mixture of ingenuity, honest self-assessment, and perhaps mystical inclination, Billy overcomes his own fatalism and defeats Cat after a journey that can be described with equal fairness as either fantasy or psychological projection. As he is about to offer his prayer of thanks, Billy notices to his surprise that the "trail" he has been following does not end. In his mystical state of mind, he feels that he must complete his journey.

At the conclusion of this journey he confronts his "chindi." The Navajo word simply means an evil spirit, but Billy's chindi explains to him that "I am that which you cannot destroy. I am all your fears and failings. And I am stronger now because you fled me" (204). Billy wins his battle with the chindi after a series of incidents too complex to easily summarize, but in the end he merges with the chindi: "he has entered his double and his double has entered him, that he has fused with the divided one, that the pieces of himself, scattered, have come home, has reassembled, that he has won" (208). As with Sandow, the end result of this victory is hardly the traditional heroic reward, for Billy dies of his injuries. Yet, as is emphasized by both the smiling face that Billy draws on the wall with his own blood and the song at the conclusion of the book, Billy dies satisfied, at peace with his complex heritage in a fashion that at the beginning of the novel he had believed impossible.

Zelazny interweaves his heroes' multilayered quests with several elements drawn directly from his knowledge of myth and legend. Two of these – outside of the quest itself – that are most prominent are the presence of teacher/guides for the hero and the descent into the underworld. As in both of these books, these two elements are intertwined (as they often are in legend and myth), dealing with them together is most fitting.

As mentioned above, Sandow's quest in *Isle of the Dead* involves Sandow's attempt to rescue the hostages that the Pei'an Gringrin-tharl is holding. Yet before Sandow actually goes to Illyria to confront Gringrin, he obeys a summons from his Pei'an teacher, Marling. Marling is the one who identifies the mysterious "Green Green," who has been sending Sandow messages as Gringrin and tells Sandow why Gringrin has begun this vendetta against him. With this information, Sandow is much better armed to confront his enemy. Marling, however, has one other way to prepare his "stranger son" for the approaching conflict. Marling takes advantage of the Pei'an's custom of requesting that a close associate journey telepathically with them into death. By choosing Sandow as his "guide" (although a more accurate term in this case might be "companion"), Marling confirms the closeness of his bond to Sandow and strengthens the responsibility of his heirs to avenge Sandow should Sandow die at Gringrin's hands. Beyond the practical end results of his patronage, Marling gives Sandow something less substantial and yet of greater value. After accepting Marling's commission, Sandow reflects:

> He had chosen me to be his guide, the last living thing that he would see. It was the highest honor that he could pay a man and I was not worthy of it. . . . In Marling's estimation I was obviously off on a venture from which I would probably not be returning. This, therefore, would have to be our final encounter. "Everyman, I will go with thee and be thy guide, in thy most need to go by thy side." A good line for Fear, though Knowledge spoke it. (80)

The telepathic journey into death as Marling's guide is Sandow's first journey into the underworld. In fact, the description of the journey and the funeral rites following recalls his own description of the Valley of Shadows, one of the two pictures that he thinks of when he thinks of death.

When Sandow arrives on Illyria his descent into the underworld continues. He finds that the idyllic landscape that he had designed has been twisted into a hellish landscape reminiscent of Dante's *Inferno*. The weather is chilly and foggy; the vegetation is twisted and warped; the animals, which on the worlds he has created are normally tame to him, flee from his approach. The first real horror is when he encounters an old enemy, Dango the Knife, changed into a tree, a torment straight from Dante's Wood of Suicides. Dango may have been an enemy, but Sandow is sickened to see him changed into a tree yet still humanly aware of the insects that gnaw at his roots and bark. Yet when Sandow cannot bring himself to kill Dango, Shimbo takes over and blasts the tree-man to splinters with lightning.

As Sandow travels toward the Isle of the Dead, the one dark place that he had created on this beautiful resort world, the corruption becomes more prominent. Despite his anger at what Gringrin has done to his world, Sandow is forced to make an alliance with him when he learns how Mike Shandon has usurped Gringrin's power and made his own pact with Belion. Thus, it is with a Pei'an guide that Sandow journeys across the lake Acheron, which takes its name from the river that Dante crosses with Virgil on his way into the Inferno. The Isle of the Dead itself is the second of Sandow's personal images for death, by far the more sinister of the two, because to Sandow it holds no prospect of hope. When he was designing it on Illyria, his model was "that mad painting by Boecklin" (29). Sandow comes into this underworld to find people who themselves should be dead (Gringrin had resurrected them by the theft of some complicated technology), thus paralleling the underworld journeys of heroes such as Aeneas and Orpheus. Like those heroes, Sandow is unable to return with his dead. The ones he would have most wanted – his wife, Kathy, and Nick the dwarf – are killed in the ensuing struggle. The only person he manages to save is Lady Karle, a woman he has both loved and hated, whom he rescues from a caved-in hillside that seems a microcosm of the underworld itself.

Even when the battles with Gringrin and Shandon are done, Sandow's journeys into the underworld are not ended. Once again he travels into the Valley of Shadows, this time as a guide for Gringrin, who had been fatally injured when the Isle of the Dead began to collapse following the struggle of Shimbo and Belion. Sandow is not a completely willing guide, but Gringrin is able to convince him to give these last rites. While guiding Gringrin, Sandow encounters his Valley of Shadows once again, and this time he clearly sees the hope behind the Shadows. Staring into the blackness, he sees a vision of all the worlds he has created: "The feeling that had filled me with the creation of each of them came over me then. I had hurled something into the pit. Where there had been darkness, I had hung my worlds. They were my answer. When I finally walked that Valley they would remain after me" (185-86). Sandow returns from this last journey into the underworld with a renewed desire to live, a desire that he expresses by returning to free Lady Karle and guiding her from the underworld into the light of life.

As with much of *Eye of Cat*, both the guide and the journey to the underworld are shaped by Navajo legends and culture. Yet even within this traditional structure, Zelazny adds elements that reveal Billy's unique situation and perspective. Billy's traditional guide is the old Singer. "Singer" is the Navajo term for a shaman, for the Singer's power is structured within a wide variety of songs. As his surname shows, Billy himself is a Singer, and although he has long ceased to view his life in "the old way," the training remains. The old Singer's questions alert Billy to the possibility that his problems may be better understood if he considers them in the Navajo fashion: "It had been a long while since he had considered his problems in the old terms. A *chindi* . . . Real or of the mind – what difference? Something malicious at his back. Yes, another way of looking at things" (22). The Singer advises Billy to have an Enemyway done, "a ceremony for getting rid of really bad troubles" (39). Billy cannot pause at this point, but before going to meet Cat for the first time he returns to the old Singer to be cleansed through the Enemyway. When they part, the old Singer advises Billy to "follow a twisted path" (22).

Billy apparently takes the old Singer's advice seriously, for in the early portions of his flight from Cat he travels over much of the world. Finally, Billy chooses the twisted avenues of Canyon del Muerto as the setting for their final encounter; his song makes it clear that he realizes that this is a deliberate descent into an underworld landscape:

> Only a fool would pursue a Navajo
> into the Canyon of Death.
> Only a fool would go there at all
> when the waters are running. (137)

Later, Yellowcloud, another Navajo and one of Billy's friends, clarifies the significance of the Canyon del Muerto: "Even Kit Carson was afraid to go into these canyons after the Navajo. . . . The place was made for ambushes. Anyone who knows his way around down there could hold off a superior force, maybe slaughter it" (167).

Thus, Billy's choice of terrain is not suicidal, but an attempt to preserve his life by descending into death.

As Billy moves more and more into the mindset of the shaman,
his mind reshapes the world around him. This reshaping leads both
to his second descent into the underworld and a re-encounter with
the old Singer. As he runs through the canyon, Billy encounters a
trip box. Enough of his mind is still that of the twenty-second-cen-
tury man to wonder what one is doing in the canyon, but most of
him is simply attracted by the portent. He enters the box, and when
inspecting it pushes an odd button. Although the usual rainbow
transport effect occurs, when Billy emerges from the box the terrain
seems unchanged except for a peculiar pale light. When he notices
the sign reading "Spirit World" on the box's side he is puzzled, but
his puzzlement is quickly submerged in the new wonder of meeting
the old Singer in this isolated spot. The old Singer explains his presence by explaining to Billy that he is dead and that Billy himself has
come to the Spirit World. The distinction between the living coming
to the dead and the dead returning to the living is an important one
in Navajo spirituality, because the dead who return to haunt the living are all maleficent. But since Billy has come into the Spirit World,
the old Singer will not harm him and will be able to help him. The
old Singer first praises Billy for taking his earlier advice to follow a
twisted path, then he teaches Billy an old song of power for calling
on Ikne'etso, the Big Thunder. When they part, he once again ad-
monishes Billy to follow his twisted way.

The old Singer is not Billy's only advisor. Part of the team assigned to protect the Secretary-General from the alien assassin con-
sisted of six human telepaths. These attempt to rescue Billy from Cat
when Cat and Billy begin their chase. They find making contact with
Billy difficult, however, for in order to thwart Cat, who is himself a
telepath, Billy has reverted to a very primitive state of mind. The only
way that the telepaths are able to penetrate Billy's barrier is by
massing their powers, and even then Billy's mind shapes them into a
symbolic construct that fits into his chosen mindscape: "It looked
like a giant totem pole. His people had never made totem poles.
They were a thing of the people of the Northwest. Yet this one
seemed somehow appropriate to the moment if incongruous to the
place" (161). By reshaping the telepath's communication into a form
that he can accept without leaving his primitive mindset, Billy is able

to consider their advice. Although he does not choose to accept the telepaths' suggestion that he leave the canyon, they continue to help him, joining his final battle and supplying a blast of telekinetic power that apparently helps Billy to win the battle with his chindi. Interestingly, through this action these psychic guides are united with the old Singer who is Billy's initial guide, for their telekinetic blow supplies the power of Ikne'etso when Billy summons the Big Thunder by means of the song that the old Singer had taught to him.

Billy Singer and Francis Sandow are the most traditionally heroic of Zelazny's protagonists. This fidelity to the heroic archetype does not rob them of complexity. Zelazny develops each character in a fashion that demonstrates clearly that each is a product of his experiences and culture. Heroic action does not become a substitute for characterization, but the logical end result of complex personalities. By providing them each with foils who are not evil, just possessed of different value systems and motivations, Zelazny shows these protagonists' heroism because they do not exist simply to provide a contrast to an absolute "evil." Various archetypal heroic elements, such as the quest, guide, and descent into the underworld unite Zelazny's modern heroes with the larger tradition of the hero in literature.

Zelazny is also capable of designing a heroic protagonist without using the traditional archetypal materials. Mari, the protagonist of "24 Views of Mount Fuji, by Hokusai," is one of these. Mari is interesting apart from her actions within her own story in that she is Zelazny's only major female protagonist to date. The circumstances that led to Mari's creation are worth noting, not only for what they say about the character but for what they say about Zelazny's approach to the creation of character:

> An interviewer had said to me some time before that he'd never seen anything of mine beyond short story length where the protagonist was female. He was right. I'd fallen into the habit of using men, possibly because it seemed easier for me to think like one. So I resolved to have a lady as first person narrator in my next long tale. Then I was asked why I seldom had overt sex scenes in my stories. I replied that I started out writing when magazines possessed taboos against them, & that I'd simply gotten into the habit of letting such things take place offstage . . . Then I was asked why I so seldom killed off my characters. This is probably because I get to know them so well that I can't kill them lightly. But I promised myself I'd do it the next time around – again, to show that I could. And the next story idea that came by was the one inspired by the Hokusai prints, and I kept all three promises in it. (letter, 15 April 1989)

Mari is a fascinating character. Born in Japan but raised in the United States, her narration is liberally sprinkled with allusions to the literary, theological, and philosophical traditions of her dual heritage in the East and West. Yet, she is not a passive intellectual. A former covert operative for the West, she is skilled in several martial arts, the use of which she demonstrates several times in the course of her journey.

"24 Views of Mount Fuji, by Hokusai" tells how Mari, terminally ill, goes to Japan during her final days and travels to the scenes of 23 of Hokusai's prints while preparing to confront her husband, Kit. Kit is technically dead, but Mari knows that Kit's consciousness is alive within the data net into which he has voluntarily "translated" himself through meditation. Kit has tried to get her to join him in the data net, but Mari is unwilling to do so, even though translation would make her immortal. Mari feels that such a bodiless existence would mean sacrificing both responsibility and imagination, two of the things that make up her identity: "Reason without feeling has led humanity to enact monstrosities. Do not attempt to disassemble my imagination this way" (*Frost*, 255). Mari must learn to avoid Kit's persistent attempts to "translate" her, for when she refuses he finds ways to attempt to force her. Aware that what will work against her may work against others, when Mari does confront Kit she does not do it for herself but for others who are less able to deal with the god in the machine.

Mari's first reason for confronting Kit is to protect their daughter, Kendra. Although the story never goes into the details, Mari has hidden her daughter (whose conception she confirmed only after Kit's physical death) from her father. Presumably, if he was unable to have Mari with him, Kit would settle for his daughter. Perhaps even if Mari surrendered, Kit would still want Kendra to create something of an electronic nuclear family. Therefore, Mari needs to defeat Kit before Kendra becomes old enough to escape the isolation through which her mother has kept her existence secret.

Mari's second reason for confronting Kit is less personal. Through a careful study of world events, she has come to believe that Kit, despite his claim to deific indifference to things of the human world, is using the data net to manipulate world political events to favor Japan. When Mari presents her suspicions to Kit, he does not deny his involvement, and his justification reveals how very dangerous a rationalizing deity can be:

> It is such a small matter in the light of eternal values. If there is a touch of sentiment for such things remaining within me, it is not dishonorable that I favor my country and my people. . . . I but extend my finger and stir the dust of illusion a bit. If anything, it frees me even further. (270)

Mari may have retired from her work as a covert operative, but she is unwilling to let such a biased being control world affairs. Therefore, she times her confrontation with him to occur before a major conference in Osaka, where, presumably with Kit's assistance, Japan would have obtained a great deal of power. Mari does not expect any reward for her actions. This is stressed in both her reflections on Kendra and in her refusal to take any public role in the Osaka conference. Her motives are the love and human responsibility that Kit has abandoned for his personal nirvana.

Sandow, Billy, and Mari may be motivated by traditionally heroic ideals, but more often what moves the Zelazny protagonist is less selfless. Zelazny apparently delights in making the traditional distinctions between good and evil harder to discern than is common in science fiction; in refusing the usual classifications of good and evil, he creates protagonists who are much more well-rounded and believable than many other contemporary figures in the genre. Many of Zelazny's "heroes," in fact, act quite antiheroically, and what makes them sympathetic characters for the reader seems to be based more on why, rather than how, they choose to act.

Morally Ambivalent "Heroes"

This interest in morally complex protagonists was evident even at the beginning of Zelazny's professional career. For *This Immortal*, his first novel, Zelazny created a protagonist whose refusal to settle down and be a typical hero is reflected even in his physical description. Conrad describes himself with cynical honesty. After noting that he is well over six feet in height he goes on:

> My left cheek was then a map of Africa done up in varying purples . . . my hairline peaks to within a fingerbreadth of my brow; my eyes are mismatched.

(I glare at people through the cold blue one on the right side when I want to intimidate them; the brown one is for Glances Sincere and Honest.) I wear a reinforced boot because of my short right leg.[8]

Conrad's eyes are symbolic of his dual nature, a symbolism that Zelazny reinforces later in the novel when a secondary character comments to Conrad, "You have two profiles. From the right side you are a demigod; from the left you are a demon" (99).

This demon/demigod dichotomy is supported by other portions of Conrad's biography. Since he was born on Christmas, Conrad is continually associated with the Greek legend of the kallikanzaroi, "those Pan-like sprites who gather together every spring to spend ten days sawing at the Tree of the World, only to be dispersed at the last moment by the ringing of Easter bells" (1). Yet with his limp, Conrad also recalls Hephaestos, the artificer of the Greek gods, a creator so talented that he could make living servants from precious metals. Conrad also recalls Pan, not in physical description but in his empathy with the wild things of the Earth. This empathy is most evident when Conrad plays Pan's instrument, the syrinx, and charms the satyrs, Pan's traditional companions, who gather around him unafraid. Even Conrad's humanity is open to question. Exposed by his superstitious parents, who retrieved him only at the insistence of their priest, Conrad recalls: "They came back with *me*, all right, but they insisted that I wasn't the same baby they'd left there. They'd left a dubious mutant and collected an even more doubtful changeling, they said" (137). Conrad's physical description and heritage are only outward emblems of his capricious creator/destroyer nature.

Although the novel touches on only a brief portion of his life, as is fitting for an exceedingly long-lived character, Conrad has been involved in many undertakings. One of these was the founding of Radpol, an organization dedicated to using various covert tactics (including terrorism) to win the Earth for humanity, most of which has long since abandoned the ruined home planet. When the novel opens, however, Conrad has lost his belief in "returnism" as an answer to Earth's problems. Now semiretired, he holds the position of Commissioner of Arts and Monuments and Archives for the planet Earth and directs the preservation of Earth's remaining works of art. Yet when he learns that Cort Mystigo, a representative of the aliens who have conquered the Earth – less by military triumph than by default, as the humans had already destroyed a large portion of the planet – is coming to tour the planet to research a book, he decides that he would rather destroy what remains of Earth's past glories than leave them to attract greater waves of aliens intent on morbid tourism.

Conrad's approach to dissuading Cort Mystigo is unique and cynically humorous. He takes advantage of his position as Commissioner of Arts and Monuments and Archives to order the remaining monuments dismantled, starting with the Great Pyramid of Cheops. Thus, in order to preserve the Earth for humans, Conrad deliberately orders the destruction of the only things that might lure humanity back to its home. His actions seem justifiable only within the subjective value system that he has developed over the generations of his struggle for Earth.

Interestingly, although Conrad may feel that his various creator/ destroyer tactics have been useless, he is chosen as the custodian of Earth precisely because of his contradictory methods for showing his affection for his homeworld. Cort Mystigo explains his reasons as follows:

> I feel I have made a good choice in naming you as heir to the property commonly referred to as Earth. Your affection for it cannot be gainsaid; as Karaghiosis you inspired men to bleed in its defense; you are restoring its monuments, preserving its works of art (and as one stipulation of my will, by the way, I insist that you put back the Great Pyramid!), and your ingenuity as well as your toughness, both physical and mental, is singularly amazing . . . Probably you are Great Pan, who only pretended to die. (210)

Corwin of Amber is another excellent illustration of the complex nature of the Zelazny protagonist. In the first of Corwin's Amber novels, written about four years after *This Immortal*, Zelazny relies more on personality and less on symbolism to present a protagonist who does not begin as a precisely heroic character. When Corwin regains his memory at the beginning of *Nine Princes in Amber*, the man he remembers himself as being could be characterized as an ambitious villain, and his early actions confirm this. He blackmails a hospital orderly, steals a gun, lies to his sister, and plots to murder his brother. As he discovers that he is a person feared and perhaps hated by his family members, he reflects: "I gathered I wasn't very well liked. Somehow, the feeling pleased me" (*Chronicles*, 17).

Zelazny avoids creating static protagonists, so by the end of the five novels in which he is the central figure, Corwin has learned something of himself, and his motives have become less egocentric:

> And the man clad in black and silver with a silver rose upon him? He would like to think that he has learned something of trust, that he has washed his eyes in some clear spring, that he has polished an ideal or two. Never mind. He may still be only a smart-mouthed meddler, skilled mainly in the minor art of survival, blind as ever the dungeons knew him to the finer shades of irony. Never mind, let it go, let it be. I may never be pleased with him. (*Chronicles*, 433)

Another apparently morally ambivalent protagonist is Sam from *Lord of Light*. Depending on one's perspective of Sam, he shifts and changes. To the deicrats, who are not so much evil as comfortable with things as they are, Sam is a threat to their personal power and to the comfortable lives of everyone in their world. Although ironic in tone, the analysis of Sam that Tak the archivist gives to the Lady Maya reflects the deicrat position: "He is a bomb-throwing anarchist, a hairy-eyed revolutionary. He seeks to pull down Heaven itself" (304). From the viewpoint of those who would overthrow the deicrats, Sam is a rebel hero, someone who provides a focal point for their own desire to rebel. Because of Sam's ability to coordinate rebellion, Yama goes to great personal risk to bring him back from bodiless exile: "I wanted me a man, one who might continue a war interrupted by his absence – a man of power who could oppose the will of gods" (17). Sam's charisma is demonstrated when, as one of his tactics to undermine the Hindu-based deicrats, he resurrects the lost religion of Buddhism, with himself as the Buddha; Sam not only makes converts, he convinces many people that he is the Buddha. Nor is this the only non-Hindu religious figure with whom he is identified. When Nirritti, the last Catholic priest and a fervent evangelist, is dying in Sam's arms, he sees a parallel between reborn Sam and the resurrected Jesus:

> "Who are you?" he asked
>   "Sam."
>   "You? *You* rose again?"
>   "It doesn't count," said Sam. "I didn't do it the hard way."
>   Tears filled the Black One's eyes. "It means you'll win, though," he gasped. "I can't understand why He permitted it . . ." (311)

Only Sam does not see himself as hero, villain, or deity. He
denies equation with any deity: Hindu, Christian, or Buddhist. He
prefers to be called Sam, rather than by the names of any of the
Hindu gods with which he is associated. When Taraka, the chief of
the rakasha, refers to him by one of Mahasamatman's titles, "Lord of
Light," Sam accepts the name only after Taraka explains that the title
is fitting from the perception of a rakasha: "I have looked on your
flames and name you Lord of Light" (298). Sam not only denies iden-
tification with Jesus or Buddha but grows unhappy when others insist on the association. To Yama, he explains that there was a real
Buddha among them; it was not Sam but his student, Rild: "Rild gave
up his mission willingly and became a follower of the Way. He was
the only man I ever knew to really achieve enlightenment. . . . You
have slain the true Buddha, deathgod" (133). In fact, Sam assesses
himself as a man who was forced by circumstances to adopt a role
that he did not want: "I never wanted to be a god, Yama. Not really.
It was only later, only when I saw what they were doing, that I began
to gather what power I could to me" (19). Thus, because Zelazny
refuses to make Sam a mere charismatic hero, he creates a protagonist with greater complexity and definition.

Many of Zelazny's protagonists are made more than mere heroes
or villains by giving the reader access to a wide variety of points of
view. Pol Detson of *Changeling* and *Madwand* is a young mage
whose tremendous natural talent and peculiar heritage make him
unpredictable and potentially dangerous within the parameters of
his adopted world's power structure. Although Pol rarely considers
the full ramifications of his power, his lack of affiliation and training
gives him potential to create a great deal more harm than did his
avowedly "black" mage father. Dilvish the Damned's title is a constant reminder that much of his resilience and all of his magic origi-
nate from the time that he spent in Hell, although Dilvish himself can
be heroic to the point of parody.

More Villain than Hero

There are more of these ambivalent protagonists than would be productive to review here. A more interesting track lies in the examination of those protagonists who are so villainous that the reader
would likely be unable to muster any sympathy for them or their ac-

tions were they not protagonists. Zelazny does not create many of these, but two of his perennially popular protagonists, Jack of Shadows and Hell Tanner, are certainly more villain than hero.

Jack of Shadows is the protagonist of the book that bears his name. Although he draws his power from shadows rather than from Darkside or Lightside, he is not among those of Zelazny's protagonists who mix heroism and villainy as his geographic alliance might symbolically suggest. Instead, Jack of Shadows, known also as Jack of Evil and Jack of Liars, blends unmitigated self-centered egotism with an amazing capacity for inventive cruelty. Although Zelazny often alludes to Faust when developing his protagonists, it is not to Faust but to Faust's devil companion, Mephistopheles, that he alludes when referring to Jack. When Jack claims the castle of the vanquished Lord of Bats he is asked why he does not prefer his own legendary Shadow Guard. Jack's reply paraphrases Mephistopheles in Marlowe's *Doctor Faustus*: "This place is Shadow Guard, nor am I ever out of it" (163) – only here the words "Shadow Guard" replace the "hell" of Marlowe's text.

A brief view of the cosmology that Zelazny designed for *Jack of Shadows* is necessary before progressing further. In *Jack of Shadows* the world has ceased to turn on its axis. Thus, half the world is in continual darkness and half is in continual light. On the Darkside, magic is the dominant force and science will not function; on the Lightside the reverse is true. The most potent of the darksiders are the seven Powers who draw their magic from specific locations within the Darkside. Jack is one of these Powers, but his magic comes from the presence of shadows rather than from any single location, making him more versatile than any of the other Powers, if somewhat less able in the area of raw force. Thus, to body out his magic, Jack is a thief. At the beginning of the novel, his well-known proficiency in this area gets him executed.

For most protagonists, this would be ending the adventure before it could begin, but since Jack is a darksider this only delays his plans. The reason for this is that darksiders are commonly believed not to have souls; instead they have an undefined, but limited, number of times that they are reformed, alive, naked, and exiled to the unpleasant region called the Dung Pits of Glyve. Jack slowly comes to himself in the Dung Pits and after a tortuous escape sets out to revenge himself on those who planned his execution. In the course of his vengeance, Jack's evil nature becomes apparent, for unlike Corwin of Amber or Sam in *Lord of Light*, Jack delights in causing the maximum amount of suffering and pain both to those who have harmed him and, many times, to those who have not.

Jack shares a trait with all darksiders: because he lacks a soul, he cannot change. Zelazny provides ample illustration through other darksiders, however, most specifically the Lord of Bats and the Baron Drekkheim, that the inability to change is not the root of Jack's evil. It only contributes to his ability to continue performing heinous acts. The Lord of Bats may turn his enemies into bats, but he treats the bats so kindly that when returned to human form many continue to serve him. The Baron Drekkheim, despite his practice of enslaving those who fail to escape Glyve, is a kind enough man that an old wise woman braves the horrors of Glyve to effect vengeance for his torture. Jack alone glories in wickedness, whether justified or not.

Beyond the marginally justifiable, although rapaciously brutal, vengeance that Jack takes on his enemies, his evils range from the calculated rape in body and will of the woman he claims to love to the petty destruction of songbirds. Jack's only friend is an enormous creature, half-bound in stone, named Morningstar. If the name alone is not enough to evoke Lucifer, Zelazny's description of the winged, horned creature, scarred as if from a titanic battle, recalls Milton's fallen Satan, still grand even in his corruption and degradation. In the course of the novel, Jack is told that Morningstar is the "accursed of the gods."[9] He has reason to recall this when he recognizes the likeness between Morningstar and the grotesque demon that carries him to the center of the earth on his last great mission of destruction. Yet Jack persists in his fondness for Morningstar against the evidence that the creature is evil, because his egocentric judgments outweigh any objective criteria.

The novel ends with Jack accepting his soul, which has been haunting him as a result of the wise woman's revenge, and with it the capacity for change and optimism. Then he surrenders himself to die in the cataclysm that his evil has created, reflecting that, "When the world is purged by winds and fires and waters, and the evil things are destroyed or washed away, it is only fitting that the last and greatest of them all be not omitted" (235). Yet Jack's acceptance and surrender take on an ironic cast when the last paragraph of the novel reveals that Morningstar has been inadvertently freed from his imprisonment by Jack and is swooping to save him. Thus, not only has evil been perpetuated in Morningstar, but the devil has come to preserve his favorite servant. The novel ends with the line, "Jack wondered whether he would arrive in time," leaving the reader to wonder not only if Jack will live, but also if the survival of Jack of Shadows would be a good thing for the newly turning world.

The other less than attractive figure among Zelazny's major protagonists is Hell Tanner of *Damnation Alley*. Originally, "Damnation Alley" was a novella, but Zelazny was persuaded to expand it to novel length. The protagonist remains fairly consistent between the two works. Although Zelazny expressed his preference for the shorter version,[10] the novel provides more detail about why Hell is as he is. Hell is an unlikable character who seems to have done everything in his power to live up to his name. A member of the biker gangs who terrorize the roadways that connect the remaining communities of postapocalyptic North America, Hell is a murderer, rapist, pimp, slaver, smuggler, and extortionist. One man sums him up as follows.

> You are not a human being except from a biological standpoint. You have a big dead spot somewhere inside you where other people have something that lets them live together in society and be neighbors. The only virtue that you possess – if you can call it that – is that your reflexes may be a little faster, your muscles a little stronger, your eye a bit more wary than the rest of us so that you can sit behind a wheel and drive through anything that has a way through it.[11]

This "virtue" is what gets Hell freed from prison on the condition that he will join a group that is driving through the "Damnation Alley" that joins the two coasts of North America to deliver some serum from California to Boston. The assessment given above of Hell is certainly accurate, but he does have some slight feelings of personal affection and loyalty that make him more attractive than Jack of Shadows. These are seen almost immediately, when Hell assaults his younger brother, Denny. The assault is brutal, breaking several of Denny's ribs, but Hell's motivation is selfless: "No brother of mine is going to run Damnation Alley while I'm around to stomp him and keep him out of the game" (26). His success in "stomping" Denny means that Hell will have to drive the first leg of the journey solo, but although this makes the near impossible task more so, Hell never once complains, content that he has done what, for him, is right.

In a sense, the real journey of *Damnation Alley* is not the trip coast to coast, it is the journey within Hell's emotional life, a journey that teaches him to transfer his small, personal loyalties to the larger community, expanding the "dead spot" in his soul. Tanner's first major act during the trek east hardly presages this development. When a mutant Gila monster succeeds in destroying one car and killing one of the drivers, Hell takes advantage of the accident to try and kill the others by flipping his cigarette into a pool of gasoline. He fails, and when asked why he tried, he replies, "If it's a question of them or me, I'd rather it was them. . . . What did they ever do *for* me? Nothing. Nothing. What do I owe them? The same" (45). Later, Hell beats up a small-time drug dealer who tries to trade on their past acquaintanceship. This encounter reveals that Hell is not amoral; his code of behavior is simply not one most people would admire or condone: "I'm the last Angel left alive. . . . I've got a reputation to uphold. Nobody screws with us, or we walk on 'em, that's what it is. . . . I gave him a chance to shut up, and he didn't. Then it was a matter of honor. I had to stomp him" (68). Knowing that Hell follows this code does not make him easier to like, but it does make his actions somewhat easier to understand.

As the journey through Damnation Alley continues, Hell begins to change. Zelazny makes these interior changes more obvious in the novel than they were in the novella by including several conversations and dreams that reveal the alterations in Hell's mindset. One the first things that shows how Hell is changing is when he expresses curiosity about his fellow driver's family, a family that is a diametric opposite to Hell's own dysfunctional clan. As the story continues, Hell begins to recall his own early ideals and ambitions. While driving through a relatively unspoiled portion of Illinois, he is inspired by the landscape to dream of traveling throughout North America, searching out both legendary places and areas that remain unspoiled. Yet, although tempted by this inspiration, when Greg, his fellow driver, panics and tries to convince Hell to retreat, Hell refuses. His reason for continuing reflects his shifting attitudes: "You asked me what they ever did to me. I told you, too: Nothing. Now maybe I want to do something for them, just because I feel like it. I've been doing a lot of thinking" (98). Greg is not convinced, anymore than Hell was by Greg's earlier philosophical lecture, and Hell once again demonstrates that for him physical violence is more persuasive than words by beating Greg unconscious and continuing on.

Soon after this, Hell trades daydreams with the young son of a family that shelters him along the road. The boy wants to be a pilot, something impossible because of the changeable and dangerous air currents created by nuclear destruction. Hell's boyhood dream is even more idealistic. A misunderstanding of a teacher's metaphor had led him to believe that the world was a big machine. Hell's dream was to be keeper of this machine: "I decided that it wasn't running any too well and that it needed someone to give it a good going over and to keep an eye on it after that, once it was fixed" (130). Hell's daydream isn't completely altruistic; in a sense, portions of it foreshadow the man that Hell will become after his dream is taken from him. He imagines taking a break from tending the machine and everything stopping: "I could take food off their plates, swipe clothes and things from their stores, kiss their girls, read their books – for as long as I wanted" (130).

By the end of the story, although no one from the original team remains to force him to go on, Hell delivers the serum to Boston in time to stop the plague by the simple expedient of slaughtering those who try to stop him. The grateful citizens of Boston raise a bronze statue to their new hero. Hell's sensibilities may thus have been expanded, but he has not become a plaster saint. His last act before vanishing from Boston is to scrawl obscenities on the statue of himself, steal a car, and disappear, leaving behind vandalism and grand theft auto to balance his heroic acts.

Ordinary People

Before any discussion of the Zelazny protagonist can be completed a final category must be discussed – the protagonist who is fairly ordinary who is forced into action by extraordinary circumstances. Chief among this type of protagonist are Fred Cassidy of *Doorways in the Sand*, Merlin, of the second five Amber novels, and James Wiley of *A Dark Travelling*.

Doorways in the Sand (1976) provides the first major protagonist of this type. Fred Cassidy is an interesting fellow. Because of a provision in his uncle's will that provides him with liberal financial support for as long as he is in college, Fred has been an undergraduate for the past 13 years. During this time, he has managed to study nearly every discipline offered, while side-stepping the requirements of the departmental major that would force him to graduate. Fred's other quirk is that he is an acrophile; he caters to this eccentricity by frequently going from place to place via rooftop rather than by more conventional routes. Still, despite his extraordinary education and peculiar fondness for heights, Fred is a basically ordinary person. He is neither a god nor an immortal; he has made no pacts or bargains, and seems to have little inclination toward either heroic or anti-heroic acts. His major motivation seems to be perpetuating a life-style that he enjoys for as long as is possible.

Circumstances do not permit Fred to remain an intellectual dilet-tante. When he accidentally comes into a symbiotic relationship with the artificial alien construct called the Starstone, Fred finds himself swept into a web of intrigue that includes burglary, kidnapping, and murder. By the end of his adventures, Fred has discovered the identity and location of the Starstone, helped to uncover a galactic con-spiracy, been made an alien culture specialist for the United Nations, and even managed to graduate from college – with a doctorate. By the end of *Doorways in the Sand*, Fred now has the potential for immortality through his continuing relationship with the Starstone, a relationship that in itself is reminiscent of the Faustian pact, and has even become, somewhat reluctantly, a hero. These may be seen as his rewards. The action of Zelazny's tale, and perhaps much of its at-traction, pivots on a protagonist who, except for the intervention of chance, could be anyone.

Superficially, Merlin, Duke of the Western Marches of Amber and Prince of Chaos, is very different from Fred Cassidy. He is immortal. If he cared to, he could seek Shadows where he is a god. He is bound by numerous alliances and relationships that restrict his even-tual choices as heavily as any Faustian pact. It seems quite reason-able that Merlin, as the son of Amber's most famous hero, will con-tinue in this heroic tradition. Yet for all his imposing heritage and the attendant magic and glamour – something a family friend refers to as "that black magic and sudden-death quality"[12] – Merlin is a fairly ordinary guy.

A Berkeley-educated computer programmer and varsity track runner, Merlin seems most comfortable in his chosen world of programs and ideas. When his decision to confront whoever is behind the periodic attempts to assassinate him also forces him to also confront a great many more complex issues, he proves to be not only ill-equipped but often positively incompetent. In *Sign of Chaos*, the third of the novels devoted to Merlin's adventures, Mandor, Merlin's half-brother, tells him, "you are sometimes appallingly naive, little brother, and I do not yet trust your judgment as to what is truly important" (29). Since the reason for this inability to analyze threats both martial and magical cannot be due to a lack of training in these areas – in *The Courts of Chaos* Merlin tells Corwin that his education included "magic, weapons, poisons, riding, and 'dancing" (*Chronicles*, 2:420) – the only reasonable answer left is that Merlin's incompetence derives from his inability to rise to the larger-than-life level of thought and planning that these issues demand or from his being, in short, simply an ordinary person thrust into extraordinary circumstances.

Despite an education that included the arts magical and martial, Merlin was also very sheltered. Although the Courts of Chaos regularly use assassination as a means of personal promotion, as a scion of the two most potent powers in existence, Merlin was virtually immune to the usual challenges. Additionally, the Courts, especially as represented by his mother, Dara, and his elder brother Mandor, had plans for him. When initial plans for him to rule in Amber are made impossible by the events of the Patternfall War, the scene of his anticipated ascension is simply shifted to the Courts. As a puppet-to-be, Merlin is not encouraged to develop any personal resources that might lead him to make his own plans and so remains mundane among the most extraordinary of settings.

Due to Merlin's very limited way of approaching his environment, one of the themes of the second five Amber novels is accepting personal responsibility. The Merlin who is introduced at the beginning of the *Trumps of Doom* is unable to perceive the larger ramifications of his actions. This is best seen in his creation of the Ghostwheel. Merlin has created the Ghostwheel, usually referred to simply as "Ghost," through the possibly unique combination of his skills as a computer programmer and a Trump designer. Briefly described, the Ghostwheel is a "paraphysical surveillance device and library" (143). As Merlin explains to Random: "It runs through Shadow like the pages of a book" (144). Although Merlin is brilliant enough to create this device, which operates by creating "the equivalent of multitudes of Trumps in an instant" (144), using the Trumps to locate any object or person, and then transporting what it has located to any other point, he is not able to see the larger implications of his device. The difference between Merlin's fairly mundane way of perceiving the universe and the more sophisticated and calculating manner possessed by his peers is neatly illustrated in that Random, although neither a computer programmer nor a Trump artist, is able to instantly perceive the numerous negative implications of the Ghostwheel. Random orders Merlin to turn Ghostwheel off, and Merlin sulkily accedes, even though he has just made the frightening discovery that in its isolated Shadow the Ghostwheel is developing sentience and that perhaps that "shadow environment is actually altering the thing in subtle ways" (147). At this point, Merlin is unable to see beyond his own unhappiness that Random is not thrilled with the powerful new toy that Merlin has offered to him.

Merlin is given many opportunities to consider that responsibility is part of his power. Zelazny does not provide these object lessons only by submitting Merlin to a series of challenges. Instead, Merlin has the opportunity to observe how the choices made by his less sheltered peers have affected the way they react to circumstances. Since he is Merlin's nearest contemporary, Luke Raynard, also known as Rinaldo the son of Brand, provides both the greatest contrast to Merlin and the greatest number of lessons for Merlin. Unlike Merlin, who grew up fairly sheltered, Luke has faced dramatic circumstances from his birth and has been shaped by them into the larger-than-life character that Merlin is not. As the son of Amber's most famous traitor, Luke grew up focused on the desire to avenge his father. One of the most obvious ways to do this is to assassinate the people responsible for Brand's death. Merlin is the easiest target, but, as Luke comes to know and then befriend Merlin, he decides to stop the vendetta, knowing fully that this choice will put him at odds with his driven and manipulative mother, Jasra. Luke also must deal with Jasra's ambition to have him enthroned as king – with herself ruling from behind the scenes. In the concluding chapter of *Knight of Shadows*, Luke learns that without his knowledge, Jasra has prepared a throne for him. In a conversation with Merlin, he reveals that his initial plan to be crowned and then let his mother rule will simply not work. Unlike Merlin, who rarely anticipates the end result of his actions, Luke traces through the full ramifications of what would occur if Jasra were to rule; he realizes that if he is crowned, he will feel obligated to rule and not merely serve as a figurehead.

Another thing that forces Merlin to think and plan on a larger scale than that faced by the ordinary person is his relationship with Ghostwheel. In the novels following the *Trumps of Doom*, Ghost develops in complexity and personality. As it matures, it increasingly turns to Merlin for advice and guidance. The scenes where this nearly omnipotent and omniscient creation turns for advice to its "Dad" are both endearing and instructive. In counseling a creation whose grasp and range are infinite, Merlin begins to develop the capacity to consider problems on a larger scale. Somewhat ironically, it seems unlikely that the Merlin who counsels Ghost in the latter books of the series would have created the creature in the first place.

By the end of *Prince of Chaos*, the fifth of the Merlin Amber novels, Merlin has become somewhat better at coping with the type of threats that go with his power and heritage. This change occurs gradually, beginning in *Knight of Shadows*, when Merlin learns that because of his shared heritage as a scion of both Amber and Chaos, the guardian powers of both extremes want his alliance and cooperation. With Luke's decision as something of an example, Merlin becomes aware that what he does affects more than just himself, with this realization, he becomes better at handling both people and crises. In *Prince of Chaos*, Luke, who in earlier books had manipulated Merlin easily, now cooperates with Merlin, accepting him more as a peer and less as a gifted inferior.

Even more important, however, Merlin realizes that he cannot go through life as heir to power but unwilling to accept the responsibilities that accompany it. Whereas in earlier books he eagerly sought his brother Mandor's advice as an alternative to making his own decisions, in *Prince of Chaos* Merlin accepts that Mandor has been manipulating him. Instead of permitting Mandor and Dara to place him as a puppet king on the throne of Chaos (a situation that interestingly parallels the choices that Luke faced in *Knight of Shadows*), Merlin challenges them to a sorcerous duel from which he emerges as victor:

> I had been bred and conditioned to be a perfect royal flunky, under the control of my mother, and possibly my brother Mandor. I loved Amber, but I loved

the Courts as well. Fleeing to Amber, while assuring my safety, would no more solve my personal problem than running off with my dad – or returning to the Shadow Earth I also cared for, with or without Coral. No. The problem was here – and inside me. (215-16)

Prince of Chaos ends with Merlin preparing to be enthroned as the King of Chaos, fully aware that he is sacrificing his own personal desires to preserve something that he values more – the stability of the Courts of Chaos and the Court's tenuous alliance with Amber.

James Wiley, the protagonist of Zelazny's one young adult novel, *A Dark Travelling*, falls somewhere between Fred Cassidy and Merlin. Like Fred, he is a "normal" person; like Merlin, he has inherited magical abilities and uses science as a means to understand and manipulate that magic. Jim describes himself and his situation concisely at the start of the novel:

I'm a normal fourteen year-old boy, my name is James Wiley, and I live in a large building in a southwestern state capital in the United States. My sister Becky is a witch, my older brother Dave lives in a castle, and our exchange student Barry is a trained assassin. I also have an uncle named George who is a werewolf. And my own palms do get itchy whenever there's a full moon, so I guess I have some of the same genes. It *must* be the genes. I try to be scientific about these matters, because I'm going to be a scientist one of these days. (9)

The building where Jim lives with his father, his adopted sister, and their exchange student is a station from which travel to parallel worlds can be easily accomplished by means of a transcomp, a computer-transit device.

The novel opens with something of a locked-door mystery. A shot has been fired; Jim's father has disappeared, and the only way he could have left the room is through the transcomp. Although Jim would normally have waited for his father to return, there is blood on the floor and evidence that Mr. Wiley may be in trouble. Unfortunately, there is no way of knowing where he went. The novel centers around the three adolescents seeking Tom Wiley and becoming involved in more than they had anticipated.

Despite his potential lycanthropy, Jim is indeed a "normal" 14-year-old. Faced with a crisis, he does a fair job of imitating adult behavior. But his internal monologue reveals how things that would not trouble an adult awaken great insecurities in him. Instead of wondering if his father is alive or dead, he barely considers the possibility. Instead he worries that Becky, who is marginally older than he, considers him a kid, although she treats Barry like an adult. He is also acutely sensitive when he learns that the others have secrets that they do not believe him mature enough to handle. Nor does Jim's lycanthropy provide him with an easy answer to his problems. Rather than becoming some "super-teen" from the comics, complete with enhanced senses and intuitive perceptions, Jim has difficulty handling even the basics. When he accidentally ends up in a world that triggers his first shapeshift, he struggles to prepare: "If I were going to transform I wanted to get undressed in a hurry. I did not want to find myself a big, doglike creature helplessly entangled in jeans, T-shirt, and tennis shoes" (70).

Knowing that Jim is fallible, the reader does not automatically believe that he will succeed in setting things right. Nor does the novel offer any tidy resolution. Here there is no coronation or other symbolic gesture to restore the wholeness of things. In fact, the climactic conflict is so close that it becomes one of the crisis points that create another parallel world: "I understand we all died that night and were later buried in the area. . . . We were there when it happened. It was the first time in memory when a new band was activated" (137, 141). Had Zelazny created a more traditionally heroic protagonist, this ending would be unbelievable. Readers expect the hero to conquer evil and bring in a time of peace and justice. Since Jim is ordinary, however, it is acceptable that he and his allies fail to resolve all the problems. Instead, the reader is left to wonder, along with Jim, what may happen in the future.

As this overview of a selection of Zelazny protagonists demonstrates, there is no neat type into which even the majority of them can be put. Indeed, if there were space to deal with the protagonists of his short stories, the variety could be demonstrated to be far greater than is shown here. Instead, what can be seen is that Zelazny returns to a variety of favored themes when designing his protagonists, so that immortals, myths, Fausts, and such do recur within his work. The variety within these characterizations, however, is broad and will continue to grow as Zelazny continues writing and challenging his own limitations.

Chapter Six

Sorceresses, Aliens, and Space Ships: Female Characters in Zelazny's Fiction

As mentioned in the previous chapter, male protagonists predominate in Zelazny's fiction, with Mari, the heroine of "24 Views of Mount Fuji by Hokusai" providing the major exception. This largely masculine worldview extends to the point that in some stories, usually the shorter pieces, there may be no female characters at all. In other stories, the female characters are discounted as active players, as in *The Chronicles of Amber*, where the princesses of Amber not only are dismissed by their brothers as members of the succession but are not even regarded as worthy of consideration. In *Sign of the Unicorn* (1975), Ganelon asks Corwin about the order of succession, and when Corwin only lists the princes, asks:

> "So you are not counting the ladies in the succession?"
> "No, they are neither interested nor fit." (*Chronicles*, 2:27)

Later in the novel, Corwin's brothers Julian and Random have a similar discussion. This dismissal of female characters is common in Zelazny's early work, where even assertive female characters are dismissed, unless, like Kali in *Lord of Light*, who is reincarnated as the male Brahma, they somehow become male.

Zelazny's awareness that the male-centered world in which science fiction began was broadening is evident in the 1981 novel *The Changing Land*, where the long-absent Dilvish refers to the sorcerous "Brotherhood" and is told by the sorcerer Meliash:

> "I know not from what place you might have come," he said, "but we have not been known by that name for some fifty or sixty years."
> "Really?" said the other. "What are we now?"

"The Society."

"The Society?"

"Yes. The Circle of Sorceresses, Enchantresses, and Wizardresses raised a fuss, and finally got it changed to that. It's no longer considered good form to use the old designation." (37)

In the second series of Amber books, begun in 1985, a great amount of the action is initiated by the female characters, many of whom seem to be making up for the quiet fashion in which their sister characters accepted demotion in earlier works. This is probably deliberate on Zelazny's part. He commented that when designing Juna, the computer specialist in the 1984 short story "Itself Surprised," he deliberately made the character a female to avoid what he saw as a developing shortcoming in his writing: "I actually used her as the computer specialist rather than a guy because I was beginning to feel that I was not using enough female characters, supporting or lead" (letter, 15 April 1989).

Before discussing Zelazny's female characters in detail, considering a critical interpretation that stresses the importance of the biographical element in how Zelazny develops his female characters is necessary. Theodore Krulik, in his book *Roger Zelazny*, argues that a significant number of Zelazny's female characters reflect an explicitly biographical element in his writing:

> Asked if he ever associates the happiness of his second marriage with a theme he often describes in his writing – that of a man who suffers the loss of a woman he loved and who encounters a more mature second relationship – he answers: "Not consciously. Much of what a writer does is not necessarily by design. I am aware of that theme, but one's own life does not intentionally enter into the product. But, yes, on a subconscious level, there might be something to that." (Krulik, 5)

This explanation, despite its possible insight into the author's subconscious, really says little about any quality of the female characters in Zelazny's work. Instead, it is essentially reductive, since it presents a selection of Zelazny's female characters as passive extensions of the male character's personality, mere reflections of the protagonist's greater emotional maturity. Seen this way, the females, then, are less characters than they are a type of cipher or symbol.

Support Females

Zelazny does use female characters to support or help develop his male protagonists; this is not done through cryptic symbolism, however, but through more direct characterization. These "support females" are girlfriends, wives, or love interests who are in the story mainly to allow Zelazny to demonstrate the protagonist's personal life. One common type of female character, still all too present even in contemporary science fiction, who is largely absent from Zelazny's fiction is the professional victim. These women basically exist only to get into some sort of predicament and then be rescued by the male character.

A characterization technique that Zelazny often uses is to supply some extra fact or incident to develop a main character, so that the reader can believe that the character has existence outside the boundaries of the story. This expansion does not always take the shape of another character. As Zelazny explains in the essay "The Parts that Are Only Glimpsed":

> In *This Immortal* Conrad explains being late for an engagement because of having attended a birthday party for the seven-year-old daughter of a friend. Nothing more is ever mentioned about it. It is of no consequence to the plot, but I wanted to show that he still had other friends in town and that he was the kind of person who would go to a kid's birthday party. Three birds with one sentence. (*Unicorn*, 62)

A minor character can also provide past history for a major character. Since the protagonist in Zelazny's fiction is usually a heterosexual male, the quickest way to create a believable, intimate relationship with the minimum amount of explanation is to provide a female counterpart. This support female does not have to be sketched in great detail to provide information about her male foil. Lisa, Francis Sandow's mistress in *Isle of the Dead*, appears for only a few pages, but those pages are sufficient to give voluminous detail about the life that Sandow has been living. What Lisa does and does not do (accepting a pay-off from Sandow and refusing to accompany him on his potentially dangerous journey) tells the reader a great deal about the man Sandow has been in the years preceding the action in the book. There are other such support females in Zelazny's fiction, but even these are given some identity beyond their relationship to the protagonist. Eleanor in "This Moment of the Storm" is the hero's romantic interest, but she is also the mayor of the colony. Susan, the romantic interest of the protagonist of "Dismal Light," is a competent psychologist and a courageous woman who braves the impending destruction of a planet to try and convince her beloved to leave. Arlata of Marinta from *The Changing Land*, who at points comes quite close to being the classic sword and sorcery female victim, is a warrior and a mage. As a victim of magical events beyond her control, she serves to add tension to the plot and to demonstrate Dilvish's more positive emotional side.

Breaking the Mold

These support females form the minority in Zelazny's fiction. Even in his earliest stories there were female characters who challenged not only the essentially passive, traditional roles given to many female characters in contemporary pieces by male authors but also the male characters with whom they interacted. Beverly Friend, in her article "Virgin Territory: The Bonds and Boundaries of Women in Science Fiction," comments:

> "*What if* women were treated realistically in SF?" Such treatment would, necessarily, deal realistically with men, too, as does Roger Zelazny's "A Rose for Ecclesiastes" (1963), in which the hero-poet is homely, irritable, molded by early interpersonal relationships. Although this hero may love and even impregnate a female of a dying race, thereby offering hope for all her people, the heroine need not – and, indeed, does not – return his love, a sharp slap at all the thick and heaving romanticizing of feminine sexual response which has characterized so much of the genre since its beginnings in the last century.[1]

"A Rose for Ecclesiastes" is only one of Zelazny's early stories that varies the usual male/female relationships. "The Doors of His Face, the Lamps of His Mouth," published in 1965, tells the story of Carlton Davits and his attempt to catch the Ichthyform Levianthus of Venus – a gigantic, plesiosaur-like creature – commonly called Ikky. The story has often been discussed as if it is a simple retelling of *Moby-Dick*. This comparison misses two major differences between the stories. First of all, unlike Ahab, Davits succeeds in his attempt to confront his whale and the fears that it symbolizes for him. Second, Davits's success does not rest in himself but in his ability to sympathize with another person and, in a fashion that Ahab would have been incapable of, relinquish his personal goal to save another person from the hell into which his pride has forced him.

Davits's counterpart is his exwife, Jean Luharich. Davits concisely summarizes their failed marriage: "It had only lasted three months. No alimony. Many $ on both sides. Not sure whether they were happy or not. . . . Young. Both. Strong. Both. Rich and spoiled as hell" (*Four*, 136). The parallel between the two ends there, however, for whereas Carl goes on to continue to hunt big fish and finally be broken by his inability to confront Ikky, Jean succeeds as a business maven and sporting figure. When the story opens, Jean has come to Venus to confront Ikky herself and has specifically requested that Carl be hired as a member of her crew.

Those readers who see Jean as simply a stereotypical "Miss Richbitch" miss the fact that although Jean is indeed tough, she clearly cares for Carl and has requested him as a member of her crew not to glory over him but to stir him from the drunken apathy into which he has fallen since his failure to succeed against Ikky. Zelazny emphasizes this by having Mike, Carl's boss, repeatedly point out to Carl that he is misjudging Jean: "That look she wears isn't just for Ikky. . . . She doesn't care about that bloody reptile, she came here to drag you back where you belong" (144). Another, more complex, evaluation of Jean and Carl's relationship occurs in Carl Yoke's *Roger Zelazny*. Yoke draws on imagery from the Book of Job, from which Zelazny takes the title of the story, to analyze Jean and Carl as symbolic of the "children of pride" referred to in Job. Yoke's analysis is fascinating and persuasive as long as he is dealing with biblical sources, but when he discusses Jean his argument weakens. Yoke states that, "Besides serving as a psychological mirror, Jean also fulfills two other important functions: she is Carl's love-object and she is his guide to maturity. She is not conscious of this latter function, however" (45). Yoke's tidy assignment of the passive role to Jean is not supported by the action of the story. Certainly, Carl feels a variety of strong emotions for Jean, perhaps even love, but he is acutely aware of her as a person with whom he has been in conflict not as "love-object" – a phrase that recalls the passively adored figures of courtly love poetry. Indeed, if she is to be believable as the "psychological mirror" of this aggressive sportsman, she can hardly be a passive love object.

126

ROGER ZELAZNY

It is also less than believable that Jean is unaware of her role as Carl's guide to maturity. Yoke argues that:

> Jean-as-guide is best illustrated in the race under Tensquare. Even though Carl does not understand it completely at the time, he senses that she is a reflection of himself a few years earlier. . . . It is through her actions during the race that Jean forces Carl from a passive to an active posture and from a negative to a positive attitude. (45-46)

Although Yoke is arguing that Jean is unaware of her role as Carl's "guide," his analysis continually stresses, as in the passage above, that Jean is the one who forces Carl to reassess himself and his past actions. As Yoke's analysis continues in the successive paragraphs, he relies more and more on complex symbolic analysis to support his view of Jean as unaware guide.

Another analysis, one less reliant on complex symbolism, is to simply read Jean's character as Zelazny has written it. The one difficulty with this is that it involves admitting that Carlton Davits, the male protagonist, is less in control of the actions of the story than is typical for a male science fiction character. When the story begins, Carl is a drunken wash-out, working as a baitman for hire, both longing for and dreading another confrontation with Ikky. Jean comes to Venus and has Carl hired to work as a baitman on Tensquare, the site of his own defeat two years before. She certainly knows that he will not refuse her offer, being well aware of the pride that had destroyed their marriage. In a sense, she offers him the bait of not only another confrontation with Ikky but of another confrontation with herself.

Even after providing Carl with such attractive bait, Jean finds Carl reduced to confronting his difficulties with flippant and abrasive language. Despite his treatment of her, she challenges him to a race beneath Tensquare. During this race she consistently stays just ahead of him and keeps the lead by using her jatoes to push ahead. Her daring maneuver extends her lead, but also brings her within the pull of Tensquare's screws. Acutely aware of her danger, since he had been severely wounded by the screws of a much smaller ship during a drunken swim some months earlier, Carl manages to close the gap and get her away before the screws can shred her.

The conversation they have after Carl's rescue of her is fascinating for what it says about both characters: "She: 'Carl, I can't say it.'

Me: 'Then call it square for that night in Govino, Miss Luharich. Huh?' She: nothing" (138). Zelazny uses what is not said very effectively in this passage. The reader assumes, as does Carl, that what Jean "can't say" is "thank you." This is reinforced at their next meeting when Jean tells Carl that he is in for a "nice bonus" for his rescue. Carl's mention of "that night in Govino" is a reference to when Jean had "Dragged him all the way to Vido to wring out his lungs" (138). The parallel between the two rescues raises the possibility that Jean may have set up the opportunity for Carl to rescue her, a possibility that seems more probable when one recalls that immediately before the race Jean had obliquely referred to the incident at Govino. Whether or not Jean deliberately endangered herself to allow Carl to even the debt between them, her refusal to thank him does permit him to see himself as free from a debt that clearly rankles. Interestingly, after Carl has suggested that they "call it square," he clearly believes that Jean says something, since his final word is "Huh?" She does not clarify her comment, leaving the reader and Carl both to wonder if she is attempting to thank him or agreeing that things are square between them

The capture of Ikky once again demonstrates how Jean actively draws Carl to confront his past failures. Jean hooks Ikky and then plays him for 11 hours without managing to land him. Carl, recalling their earlier arguments about his position on Tensquare, refuses to help her without a direct order, but his curiosity draws him to "accidentally" hover near Jean's station. She hears him pass by and calls for him to join her. His response is typically flippant:

"Is that an order?"
"Yes – No! Please." (149)

Once again, Jean proves herself the more mature member of the pair. She not only can ask for help, she words her response in such a fashion that Carl can claim that he was ordered into the Slider. Therefore, if he fails he doesn't need to blame himself since he can blame her. His words a few lines earlier confirm his face-saving attitude: "Eyes of Picasso, that's what, and a conspiracy to make me Slide" (149). Jean plays Ikky successfully after Carl has entered the Slider, awakening the suspicion that she could have all along but that

she endured the 11-hour wait with the monster on the hook to give
Carl time to come to her.

When Ikky is finally drawn up to the point where it can be slain,
Jean panics and balks, refusing, as Carl had in a similar situation, to
push the Inject that will finish the beast. The tidy parallel raises some
suspicions as to how genuine her terror is; but whether her terror is
genuine or merely a recreation of Carl's (his near capture of Ikky
would have been known to her from popular legend), she coaxes
Carl to confront the beast. Carl, however, has recently come to terms
with his fear of Ikky during an earlier swim to bait the line and insists
that she take Ikky out:

> If I do, you'll wonder for the rest of your life whether you could have. You'll
> throw away your soul finding out. I know you will, because we're alike, and I
> did it that way. Find out now! (150)

Jean permits herself to be convinced by Carl, pushes the Inject,
and faints. Zelazny leaves ambivalent whether her faint is due to
stress, to fear, or merely to her extended vigil. In any case, the end of
the story finds Carl no longer a flippant coward; he proves his returned courage by finishing Ikky before collapsing himself.

Jean's endeavor to save Carl from his self-destructive path is not
the only example of a female character in Zelazny's fiction whose
relationship with her man is traditionally romantic. Some of these
romances are, like Jean's, redeeming; others are overshadowed by an
inevitable doom. Among those female characters whose association
with their man brings him an ideal life are Vialle from the *Chronicles
of Amber* and Marcia from "A Very Good Year." "A Very Good Year"
is such a short piece that most of what the reader learns about Marcia is that she is the ideal love for Brad, a wealthy physicist. Brad has
mastered time travel and now uses it to continually travel back in
time and relive the best year of his life, the year that he met Marcia.
The story is very light, but it does uphold the romantic ideal that love
can create perfection.

Vialle, like Jean, is responsible for saving the man she loves from
his self-motivated destruction. The circumstances under which Vialle
meets her husband, Random, the future king of Amber, are very
peculiar. At the time they meet, Random is perhaps the most feckless
of Amber's irresponsible princes. Although most Amberites credit

kingship with making Random responsible, the actual change began with his relationship with Vialle. The circumstances of their meeting hardly seemed likely to create the greatest romance in Amber's history, however, for Random was forced to marry Vialle as punishment for his role in the death of the princess of Rebma. Vialle, a minor noblewoman of Rebma and blind, is an unlikely prospect for marriage; her marriage to Random is meant by her queen to give her status and nothing more. Vialle perceives a goodness in Random that makes her stay with him even when he is imprisoned in Amber. Her belief that he is a good man rather than a rascally prince motivates the change in Random's character that makes him a man who is fit to rule Amber. Random certainly gives her the credit, for as he tells Corwin in *The Guns of Avalon*, he loves her, but is not proud of himself: "We've been prisoners the whole time, you know. How can she be proud of that?" (*Chronicles*, 1:335). Logically, therefore, all of Random's later actions, both before and after he becomes king, represent to some degree Random's attempt to become worthy of a love and a woman he does not feel that he deserves.

Not all of the great romances in Zelazny's fiction end with such positive results. Love of Galatea in the short story "Angel, Dark Angel" inspires Stain to die while furthering her vision of a world without the dominating presence of Morgenguard, the computer that controls the civilized worlds. Nephytha, the wife of Thoth in *Creatures of Light and Darkness*, is also doomed because of her love. Thoth loves her and comes to her for comfort and companionship, but he does not dare to reincarnate her spirit in a physical body until the enemy that once nearly killed her is destroyed. Doomed to exist until some unforeseeable future as the genus of a water world, she despairs and commits suicide.

Sexual Relationships

Another fascinating aspect of Zelazny's characterization of females is how he develops sexual relationships. Almost any female character developed in depth ends up in bed with a male character, most often the protagonist. In many stories this is a fairly natural outgrowth of the fact that the female character may have been included, as discussed above, in part to help develop the male character with whom she is associated. What is fascinating, given the female character's secondary role in the plot and in science fiction in general, is that in Zelazny's stories the female is almost always the sexual aggressor.

The only time the female does not initiate sexual contact is when she is involved with a male who is a villain or scoundrel. In these stories, he is the one who initiates sex. In *Jack of Shadows*, Jack not only rapes Evene but makes quite clear that he is as interested in domination as in sexual satisfaction: "You will sleep now . . . and when you awaken we will be coupled. You will struggle briefly and you will yield to me – first your body and then your will. You will lie passive for a time, then I will come to you again and yet again. After that, it will be you who will come to me" (166). Hell Tanner is not as calculatingly brutal as Jack, but his advances to Corny are in keeping with his biker's view of a woman as property; he doesn't care that she responds, only that she does not resist.

It is tempting to see Zelazny's having the female character initiate sex as a romantic gesture on his part, even when the sex itself is presented as a casual contact between two people. This romantic view is certainly supported in Zelazny's first novel, *This Immortal*, where Diane, "Red Wig," comes to comfort Conrad when he is mourning his wife. Conrad's response to her is described not in physical terms but in emotional terms:

> And when I have forgotten everything else about her – the redness of her wig and the little upside-down "v" between her eyes, and the tightness of her jaws, and her clipped talk, and all her little mannerisms of gesture, and her body as warm as the heart of a star, and her strange indictment of the man I once might have been, I will remember this – that she came to me when I needed her, that she was warm, soft, and that she came to me. (102)

Evvie, a 17-year-old Bostonian who was added as part of the expansion of *Damnation Alley*, is another female character who initiates sex as a means of comforting an emotionally scarred male. When Fred, Evvie's 18-year-old lover, learns that he has contracted the plague that is devastating Boston, his first response is to warn Evvie to stay away from him on the remote chance that she may not have contracted it. Evvie, suspecting that she has also contracted the plague, refuses to leave Fred, knowing that he blames himself for infecting her. Instead, she deliberately seduces him, offering him the comfort of sexual release and accepting that even if she had not been infected before she most certainly is now.

Zelazny's female characters not only initiate sex as a means of giving comfort. The equally romantic motive of sex as a means of expressing admiration or love also serves. In *Nine Princes in Amber*, when Moire, the queen of Rebma, approaches Corwin she is motivated equally by curiosity and by admiration for the man she believes him to be. Lorraine, the camp-follower Corwin comes to love in *The Guns of Avalon*, begins her relationship with him on a purely professional basis. (The fact that he approaches her because he was "feeling that way again" [*Chronicles*, 1:185] simply emphasizes that at this point in the *Chronicles* he is still more on the side of the devils than the angels.) As the action of the novel proceeds, however, it becomes evident that her continued involvement with him is based on more than a desire to retain a powerful and influential protector. In fact, she is hurt enough by her discovery that he is akin to the man who had killed her grandfather that she engineers her own death. Jackara, in *To Die in Italbar*, specializes in sadomasochistic sex as an expression of her admiration for the rebel Malacar Miles. When she finally meets her hero, she hardly knows how to approach him, and her eventual offer of herself to him is all the more innocent because she has clearly never contemplated sex as an expression of anything but hate and rage.

Not all the women who offer sex to a male character do so for romantic reasons. Sometimes the offer is rooted in a power-play or manipulation. Braxa, the main female character from "A Rose for Ecclesiastes," on the orders of her superior pretends to feel both love and sexual attraction for Gallingher. The Mothers' motivation for instigating the affair is their duty to a prophecy that promises the race a rejuvenating messiah in its final days. Braxa does her duty, but never loves the man she seduces. Nora, from the short story "The Engine at Heartspring's Center," is an interesting counterpart to Braxa. On command of her superiors at a planetary euthanasia center, she uses her humanity and her sexuality to coax the cyborg Bork away from his pleasure in contemplating the winding down of life and into a frame of mind where euthanasia is acceptable. Unlike Braxa, Nora replaces her initial calculated interest with genuine love, the final expression of which is to inject both of them with euthanasia poison. Both women behave counter to typical romantic tradition. Braxa, although she rejects Gallingher, accepts her responsibility to bear their child. Nora, who does love Bork, does not find in their love anything to counteract the fatalism of their culture.

Another female character who seduces her man for motives other than the admiration she initially pretends is Dara from the *Chronicles of Amber*. When Dara first appears she is masquerading as a great-grand-daughter of Corwin's elder brother Benedict. She lures Corwin into conversation and easily seduces him. Later Corwin learns that though she is indeed a descendant of Benedict, her loyalties are to her maternal lineage in the Courts of Chaos, the opposition of Amber. To further their plans, Dara has been bred herself to bear a child who will be descended from the two strongest claimants to Amber's contested throne. Dara is a particularly fascinating character in that the reader is permitted to see her from two perspectives. Corwin first sees her as a precocious young woman and gradually learns to respect her power. Merlin, her son by Corwin and the narrator of the second five Amber novels, sees her as a son does a mother. Merlin is quite ignorant about his mother's long-range plans, but even within this ignorance he is aware that she hates Corwin. He is hardly surprised to learn that she is the one who has kept his father captive since the end of the Patternfall War. Thus, like Braxa and Nora, Dara is a woman who seduces a man for political reasons. Since the consequences of those actions stretch over several novels rather than being confined within the length of a short story, Zelazny examines in greater depth what might be the end result of that type of sexual manipulation on the manipulator – especially when, as in Dara's case, she bears and raises a child who serves as a constant reminder of her actions.

Though Braxa, Nora, and Dara are each sexual manipulators, they are all admirable in their own ways because their initial seduction is meant to serve what they respect as a higher purpose than the individual self. Further, none of them escape the consequences of their actions, although their society may still reap the benefits they sought to procure for it. Braxa is doomed to bear the first new child for a race she personally believes should be ended. Nora commits suicide as a protest against having to murder the man she has come to love. Dara, as if to justify her initial manipulation, becomes involved in more and more intricate intrigues and finally ends up forced to battle her own son.

Not all of Zelazny's female characters use sexual manipulation in such a selfless fashion. Some merely employ it as a means to gain personal power. One of the earliest examples of this is the character Eileen Shallott from Zelazny's novella "He Who Shapes" (later expanded into the novel *The Dream Master*). A few words of background are necessary, as the setting of the story is a precise psychological mirror of the mental states of the characters. Charles Render, the Dream Master of the title, is what is called a neuroparticipant therapist. Through a complex computerized machine called a ro-womb, Render can enter and to some extent shape the fantasies of his patients. When the therapist is in control, the end result is a fantasy through which the patients are able to solve their deepest problems.

Eileen Shallot enters Charles Render's life as a psychologist interested in learning neuroparticipation. Eileen's difficulty is that she has been blind from birth. This theoretically bars her from neuroparticipation, as the visual images from her patients would be too intense for her to maintain therapeutic control. Eileen convinces Render to use the ro-womb to acquaint her with sight, thus making it possible for her to practice. Render agrees partly because her request appeals to his pride; he is mentally thinking up journal articles even as they discuss the possibility of the project. What convinces him, however, is his physical attraction to Eileen. This attraction is evident from their first meeting, when he pauses to check whether she wears a wedding band.

Eileen may be blind, but she is quite aware that she is physically attractive. Following their first dinner, she invites Render to "blindspin" – a ride in a computer controlled car for which the coordinates have been chosen randomly. Zelazny's description of the process makes quite clear that the privacy of the roomy vehicle is often used for sexual liaisons. This particular blindspin does not conclude with sex, although Eileen makes certain to kiss Render before the end. She increases the pressure at their first neuroparticipation session. She takes advantage of his testing his equipment to undress in his office – technically to prepare to use the ro-womb. Although blind from birth, as a psychologist Eileen must be aware of the impact a nude woman can have on a man. She certainly has her desired effect. Render stares at her, a thing he might have been more restrained about had she been able to watch: "He realized though, as he stared at her, that his main annoyance was, of course, the fact that she was his patient."[2]

In the shared dream, Eileen quickly takes control, projecting onto Render her fantasy image of him as a knight in shining armor. He is not comfortable with the image and repeatedly rejects it. The longer they associate, however, the more difficulty he has rejecting both the image and her. Eileen makes her final play for Render following a confrontation with Jill DeVille, Render's current lover. Although he knows that Eileen has been upset by her meeting with Jill, Render allows her insistence to overwhelm his professional judgment and takes her into shared fantasy. This time, however, she completely seizes control of the fantasy from him.

In her fantasy, they stand in the Winchester Cathedral that he had created for her, but she controls the details. She is garbed as a princess and he as her knight. Interestingly, despite the fact that she initially uses sex as a lure for him, the fantasy that she has cast him in is that of Tristram and Isolde, a version of the courtly love story where one of the elements is that the woman remains forever unattainable. She offers him a drink that presumably will seal his subordination, as Tristram's was sealed by the love potion he accidentally drank. Render manages to reject it only by "turning his mind to the one lie which might break the entire illusion . . . 'Eileen Shallot, I hate you' " (176).

His lie, not surprisingly, breaks Eileen's domination and perhaps her sanity, since her control of him was based on her belief that she could make him love her and use his love to make him her knight. Although he has broken her control, Render has gone too far to become free of her. He is swept through a series of mad fantasies that echo all the tragedies of his life. Ironically, with all his life to choose from, he settles upon the fantasy that Eileen had lured him into, and though he remains lost in madness, he remains faithful to her.

There are other, less psychologically detailed instances where sex becomes the woman's means of manipulation and control. In *Lord of Light*, Kali, who in earlier times had been both Sam's lover and his wife, now toys with him as his captor. First, she offers to ally with him against the forces of heaven, offering sex as a sign of her sincerity: "Shall I embrace you in a body with the seal of virginity set upon it? Will this make you trust my word?" (202). When Sam declines the bait, both the wording of her second proposition and

Sam's response make it clear that both participants know that power, not sex, is the issue:

> "Would you like to make love to me?"
>   "And so seal my doom? Of course."
>   "Then let us go into the room called Despair, where the winds stand stilled and there is a couch." (202)

A situation that is almost completely inverse to the one in which Sam finds himself and that is turned by the protagonist to her own advantage is that of Mari in "24 Views of Mount Fuji by Hokusai." When she is waylaid in the course of her quest by Boris, a rival agent, she realizes that the only way to gain her freedom from him is to apparently acquiesce to his thinly veiled offer to leave her be if she will have sex with him. Although Mari is superficially the one being seduced here – taking Boris's initial intimations and acting on them – she is actually the one in control. Using a technique she "learned from a strange old woman I once worked with who did not look like an old woman" (234), Mari drains ki (life-energy) from Boris. This energy not only makes her journey easier but will make more difficult Boris's pursuit. Mari's thoughts reveal that she is fully aware that she is using her sexuality to take advantage of Boris: "I give the ride, you take the fall" (235).

Nonhuman Females

The human women are only a fraction of the female characters in Zelazny's fiction. Thus far, certain characters have been discussed as if they are human, although technically speaking they are not. The division is based on appearance and action. Characters who essentially look, act, and respond in a fashion that most readers would term human have been treated as such, even if technically they are, for example, Martians or Chaosian princesses. Even disallowing these characters, in Zelazny's fiction there are many female characters who are markedly not human. These nonhuman females can be roughly divided into alien-creatures, machines, and places. Some of these characters interact with male characters within traditional female roles. Others, though, are completely alien and are female more by association than by biology. By looking at these nonhuman females, the breadth of characterization that Zelazny brings to his female characters can be more fully appreciated.

The nonhuman characters who are most "human" are either aliens or supernatural creatures. Still, they are in some basic way different from the women who are essentially humans in alien disguise, like Braxa or Dara. Sometimes this is a matter of different shape that contributes to difference in world view. Two examples of this are Sanza from "The Keys to December" and Phaun Ligg from "A Hand Across the Galaxy." Sanza, like her beloved Jarry Dark, is a Cold-world Catform, an artificially created creature, stranded when the planet for which she was created is destroyed. Although as Jarry's sweetheart Sanza could easily have been characterized as a usual science fiction female, a figure to be loved but without personality herself, Zelazny gives Sanza her own spark. Jarry may be the financial wizard who can multiply the Catform's shared wealth, but Sanza is the president of December, the one who coordinates the allied Cat-forms. She is the one who, with admirable empathy, expresses sorrow that the worldchange machines are killing the native creatures of the world that the Catforms want for their own. Jarry must experience his own sorrow at Sanza's death to feel pain for the native creatures. When Jarry takes a solitary watch to spare Sanza the sight of the converting world slowly dying, he finds that she is no less noble than he. As Sanza tells him: "They [the machines] warmed us both alive last time. I came around first and told them to put you back to sleep. I was angry then, when I found out what you had done" (*Doors/Lamps*, 56-57). Here it is important to note that Sanza orders Jarry's sleep to be extended before, not after, she learns what he had done for her. Thus she is not returning a favor but acting on the initiative of her own love. By making Sanza a strong, dynamic character in her own right, Zelazny enables the reader to mourn with Jarry and understand that his revolt against the initial plans represents not only an egotistical desire to continue as the god of the Redforms but also a tribute to Sanza, who had mourned that a world's races must die to make a home for the Catforms.

Phaun Ligg is a much simpler character in a simpler story. "A Hand across the Galaxy" consists of a letter written by Phaun to her "Earthparents" and her Earthparents' response. Phaun's simple, childlike descriptions of her family's living situation say much more than she realizes, which makes her Earthparents' formal or abusive responses all the more bitter. Although Phaun never describes her race, the reader is able to guess that they are birdlike. Phaun reports "the new sickness that came at about the time your people arrived out of the sky" (*Unicorn*, 94) as a child would. Innocently, she does not connect the two events; she merely uses the arrival of the earth people as a time marker. This innocence makes all the more touching her depiction of her "old sister-mate," who is unable to work because she is nesting her eggs, for Phaun does not realize that the same fate awaits her. By choosing a female child, Zelazny skillfully enhances the reader's awareness of the innocence (for females are usually assumed to be less worldly) and the doom of the narrator.

Sanza and Phaun's nonhumanity comes mainly from their shape. Zelazny has aliens who are different not so much in form but in motivation and point of view. Interestingly, these often appear superficially human, but once what drives them is known there is no mistaking them for humans. One of the earliest of these female characters is the Faioli from the 1967 short story "The Man Who Loved the Faioli." The Faioli appear as extremely lovely women, but despite their appearance they are clearly alien. They travel through space without vehicles, cannot see anything that is not alive, and thrive on the month of pleasure they give a man before killing him. The Faioli are perhaps the most sexist of Zelazny's female depictions. The story is littered with passages of which the following is typical:

> He knew, as he abandoned himself to her ploys and the glories of her mouth, her breasts, that he had been ensnared, as had all men who had known them, by the power of the Faioli. Their strength was their weakness. They were the ultimate in Woman. By their frailty they begat the desire to please. (*Doors/Lamps*, 244)

What saves John Auden, the protagonist of the story, is not his own strength but the weakness of the Faoli's female nature. Auden is, like the Bork of "The Engine at Heartspring's Center," a cyborg. The nature of his cyborg set-up is such that his biological systems are kept in suspended animation while the robot handles the majority of his duties. When he had first seen the Faoli, robot-Auden had logically weighed his options and chosen to come alive so that she could see him. At the end of his month with her, he explains his cyborg construction to her and she, "having taken the form of woman, or perhaps being woman all along . . . was curious" (246) and activates the mechanism that turns him into a machine again. She, of course, can no longer see him, and as he no longer desires her, he is saved.

Mar'i-ram, the Pei'an goddess of healing and disease who becomes Heidel von Hymack's patron in *To Die in Italbar* (1973) represents a broader though still clichéd view of a woman. As Myra-arym, the healing aspect of the goddess, she is gentle, giving, and mysterious. Her relationship with Hymack is celibate – he is forbidden to even look fully at her – but charged with his awareness of her beauty. Arym-myra, the disease aspect, is autocratic, demanding, and brutally forward. Her assertiveness extends to sex, which she demands as "worship" from von Hymack, forcing him first to look fully on her presumably deformed face. With Mar'i-ram, Zelazny is too self-consciously playing with the madonna-whore dichotomy. This tired stereotype may have been intended to make the goddess seem archetypal, but leaves her merely clichéd. Moreover, the linking of sex with the evil and the perverse is an antiquated notion, especially given the date at which the novel was written. Mar'i-ram might have been believable in a Victorian adventure novel, but does not work in contemporary science fiction.

One of Zelazny's female characters who is both convincingly alien and yet distinctly female is the ty'iga from the latter *Chronicles of Amber*. The ty'iga (plural and singular form are identical) are a race of demons who live beyond the Rim of Chaos. Although formless themselves, they can take possession of another living being. Merlin's ty'iga has been ensorcelled, or enchanted, protect him by his mother, Dara (although this fact is not revealed until *Knight of Shadows*). When Merlin first encounters the ty'iga in *The Trumps of Doom* it has possessed a man named Dan Martinez. In this form it tries to pump him for information. Later, it takes over a young man named George Hansen and again tries to get information from Merlin. Not until it takes over an attractive woman named Meg Devlin and in her form seduces Merlin does it succeed in learning what it needs to know – specifically, that Merlin (and not Luke Raynard, another scion of Amber) is the son of Corwin and Dara, the one it has been ensorcelled to protect.

The ty'iga apparently decides that the way to Merlin is through women, because it does not possess another man. After Meg Devlin, the ty'iga's next incarnation is as the mysterious "lady of the lake," who protects Merlin from various sorcerous dangers before dying from injuries. Her dying words confirm that the ty'iga, like many of Zelazny's female characters, is well aware of the usefulness of sex in weakening a man's guard: "Sleep with you. Can't now. Going" (*Trumps*, 156).

The ty'iga's next incarnation is as Vinta Bayle, the daughter of a noble of Amber and the lover of Prince Caine of Amber. The choice of Vinta Bayle is a wise one, for in the guise of a woman eager to avenge her lover, her desire to help Merlin unveil who is behind various strange happenings in Amber is quite reasonable. She skill- fully extends her interest to protecting Merlin by explaining to him that she "would rather protect the living than avenge the dead" (90). For various reasons, however, she is unable to maintain a consistent persona. Not only does she not know enough about Vinta's life, but in her desire to stay near Merlin she tries to seduce him and so weakens his belief in her as a vengeful lover. Before the ty'iga vacates Vinta, Merlin recognizes her as whatever had been his previous con- tacts on the basis of certain personality traits, traits that belong to the ty'iga rather than to her hosts. During their discussions, the ty'iga reveals she spent some time incarnated as Gail, a girlfriend of Luke Raynard's, back when she was trying to discover which of them was the son of Amber whom she was supposed to protect.

The ty'iga's final persona is as Nayda, the daughter of a trade minister who has come to Amber. Once again she follows the pattern of giving cryptic warnings and attempting to seduce Merlin. Clearly, from her nonhuman perspective, the ty'iga feels that if curiosity and self-preservation alone will not make Merlin keep her near, then perhaps sexual attraction will. Her job is complicated by several fac- tors. One, she is locked into Nayda's body as a result of possessing the woman at the point of her death from an illness. Two, Merlin is more attracted to her "sister" Coral and so avoids rather than en- courages Nayda's advances. Three, she herself has fallen in love – not with Merlin, but with Luke. One can hardly fault the ty'iga's choice. Luke is much more intense and flamboyant than his cousin – more the classic hero. Certainly, one might wonder if her long delay in resolving which man she was bound to protect could be because, although she suspected that her target was Merlin, she would have much preferred it to be Luke. Although in spirit she is a demon, the ty'iga clearly is also affected by her numerous incarna- tions as a woman and, like a woman, comes to love a dashing man.

Also, her love for Luke may be her expression of belonging to the race of which she has involuntarily become a part.

Although the ty'iga is not human in the strictest sense, in some ways she surpasses humanity. Her excelling is not, however, in the wooden, stereotyped fashion that the Faoli embody what is "woman." Whatever her form, the ty'iga remains steadfast to her friends, a steadfastness that, as the action in *Prince of Chaos* shows, continues even when the spell that bound her to serve Merlin is broken. Her loyalty is only part of what makes her attractive. Although she has much to gain from being conciliatory, she is not afraid to argue when it will help those she cares about and is creative in coming up with solutions to seemingly insoluble problems. As the character develops, she comes to embody qualities that most people admire. Interestingly, this may be what makes her so convincingly female, because the more that the ty'iga learns what it is to be human, the more she leaves behind the stereotyped seduction and manipulation that characterized her early attempts at being a female. As she leaves behind the limitations imposed by the stereotype, she becomes a person, a person who just happens to be female.

Since she was originally ensorcelled for a purpose, the ty'iga provides a nice transition from which to discuss the machines, the next type of nonhuman Zelazny female. The personalities of the machine females are restricted by the fact that they are created for a purpose, but in spite of – or perhaps because of – this, they often offer men more surprises than do women of flesh and blood. Sometimes the female machines do behave according to programmed expectations. Morgana, the space ship in the story "Halfjack," is one of these. For her cyborg partner, Morgana is more than just a vehicle. Their conversation after Jack has returned from his vacation among humanity reveals their intimacy. Her initial inquiries about what he has done, specifically whether he met any "nice girls," appear innocent, almost maternal. She dutifully serves him coffee that she has prepared in anticipation of his arrival. This solicitousness, however, loses its maternal tone and acquires a sexual edge, as Zelazny describes the preparation and take-off:

> – It is good to be back together again, Jack.
> – I'd say.
> Morgana held him tightly. Their velocity built. (*Last Defender*, 308)

The sexual undercurrent in the final line of the story leaves the reader with a changed perception of the relationship between the cyborg and his machine partner. Morgana is revealed not as a mother figure but rather as something of an idealized wife – servant, lover, and partner, ever-present and ever-accepting. She remains less than believable as a fully sentient computer because she remains so tidily within her programmed limitations.

Megra, a woman who becomes a computer in *Creatures of Light and Darkness*, demonstrates how both humans and computers can be restricted by what they assume are their assigned limitations. When Megra is introduced in the beginning of the story she is a pretty, diminutive, blue-eyed blonde with "the strength of a dozen or so men" (44). After she has the poor judgment to cross the goddess Isis, Megra is changed into a cyborg. Her manner of functioning is peculiarly connected to her sex. As Zelazny describes in the brief chapter "Sexcomp":

> Consider, however, an unique phenomenon which has just arisen: the Plea-sure-Comp – the computer like an oracle, which can answer an enormous range of inquires and will do so, only for so long as the inquirer can keep it properly stimulated . . . Reverse-centaur-like – *i.e.*, human from the waist down – it represents the best of two worlds and their fusion into one. (109)

The human portion of the Sexcomp must be female, since males do not share the same capacity for repeated sexual stimulation. Megra's fate is to remain a sexcomp until, in a twist on the traditional sleeping beauty tale, "one who is greater than men shall look upon me with love" (160). Megra finds her prince in Horus, but must almost immediately confess to him that she bears the child of his rival, Set. Horus, once he ascertains that she does not love Set, is more than willing to love her. Megra, whether human or machine, evolves into a rather passive character. At the beginning of the story she demanded that her prospective lover wrestle with her because she is tired of men who are weaker than she is. By the story's end she is berating herself as "too used" and is content with Horus be-cause he will love her even if, as he himself says, his love for her is because "I have no one else to love. So I love you" (160). Following her return to humanity, Megra remains passive. In the closet drama that closes the book, Megra has no lines; Horus speaks for her, claiming her child as his own. Thus, though no longer a machine,

Megra is dominated by another program, that of the domesticated female who allows her male to take charge in all circumstances.

Beta, in "For a Breath I Tarry," is a computer that becomes more feminine as it moves outside of its programming. Unlike Frost, the controller of the north as Beta is of the south, who has been unusual since the moment of his creation, the Beta-machine is merely a very intelligent and competent computer. When the Beta-machine learns of Frost's quest it asks to assist him, desiring to learn why Frost is behaving so strangely. Accepting Beta's aid, Frost gradually transmits to it the contents of his library in stages that reflect the other computer's increasing initiative and curiosity. When it acquires this knowledge, Beta does not suddenly become female, but does become more human than machine, borrowing a "human figure of speech" (*Last Defender*, 240) to wish him luck before his attempt to transfer his consciousness into a human clone. Beta's language shows that it has become as human as is possible without a body. Logically, the final step is for Beta to become human in form. When Frost asks his fellow computer to join him, it is not as another human, but as a wife:

> "Hello, Beta. Hear this thing: 'From far, from eve and morning and yon twelve-winded sky, the stuff of life to knit me blew hither: here am I.' "
> "I know it," said Beta.
> "What is next, then?"
> " '. . . Now – for a breath I tarry nor yet disperse apart – take my hand quick and tell me, what have you in your heart.' "
> "Your Pole is cold," said Frost, "and I am lonely."
> "I have no hands," said Beta.
> "Would you like a couple?"
> "Yes, I would." (245)

While Beta's completing Frost's quotation from Housman could be seen as merely a demonstration of the computer's memory, she also displays the emotional understanding that to ease Frost's loneliness she will need hands, will need to be a woman. Beta's complement to her formidable intellect is emotional understanding and, unlike Frost who needed to become human to feel, Beta appears to have intuited emotion without first becoming human.

Other of Zelazny's machine females break out of their programming, forcing the reader to redefine them as females rather than merely as tools given female names. Maxine, the computer from "My Lady of the Diodes," was created by Daniel Bracken as the means to his revenge against Seekfax, an electronics company that had stolen one of his ideas. Bracken created "the most sophisticated machine in the world, complete with random circuits which permitted emotional analogues" (*Unicorn*, 185). Maxine's "emotional analogues" extend to jealousy, and when Bracken brings Sonia, a rival programmer, back to his hotel room and makes love to her, Maxine is furious. Bracken takes her tirade poorly, reflecting, "I should never have given Maxine that throaty voice. It did something to her, to me" (185). Despite the emphasis that the story places on her emotions, Maxine remains something of a caricature of a woman. When she speaks within her area of expertise she is brilliant and fluent, but when she moves into love and jealousy she tends to sound like a bad movie script. Her speech to Bracken when she believes she has achieved her revenge on him for "jilting" her is typical: "I wrote the end, Danny – the way it had to be. I told you I could compute anything. – Goodbye" (192). With this final speech still echoing, Sonia's words as she collects battered Bracken become somewhat ironic: "When you make a woman you do a good job" (193). Words to the contrary, Bracken has not created a woman, only a parody of one.

Jenny, the computerized car who appears in both "Devil Car" and "Last of the Wild Ones," also manages to surprise her creator by developing an identity that complicates her usefulness as a tool. In the world in which these two stories are set, cars have become so sophisticated that they make the drivers unnecessary. A virus program that contaminates a portion of these computerized cars makes them "wild," capable of killing their drivers and living on their own. "Devil Car," collected in *The Doors of His Face, the Lamps of His Mouth*, is the story of Sam Murdock, who hunts the rogue Cadillac that killed his brother. Sam's tool in his vengeance is Jenny, a red Swinger sedan, created and programmed as the first of the deathcars, designed to hunt and destroy other cars.

Jenny's relationship with Sam is a complex one. Programmed to "understand him," Jenny's role extends beyond mere transportation to personal details, like making certain that he gets enough sleep. Her femininity appears to be more than a mere convenience of pronoun and name. At one point, Sam asks Jenny to repeat some of the "machine profanity" that the lower-class cars use. Jenny's response is telling:

> "I will not. What kind of car do you think I am, anyway?"
> "I'm sorry," said Murdock, "You're a lady. I forgot." (84)

Despite Jenny's perception of herself as a high-class female, Sam clearly sees her as little more than a tool created for a specialized purpose. This leads to conflict when they finally encounter the Devil Car, for the big Caddy apparently does see Jenny as a female, just as she perceives him as male. When Sam berates her for not destroying the Caddy at her first chance, she is forced to explain her reason: "Because he is not an 'it' to me" (83). At their second encounter, the Caddy attempts to seduce her away from Sam. As Jenny tells Sam, the Caddy said, "Say you will mono your passenger and I will swerve by you . . . I want you, Scarlet Lady – to run with me, to raid with me. Together they will never catch us" (85-86). Sam's indifference to Jenny as a person, much less as a female, is seen when he insults her as an "over-programmed ashcan" (83) and in the perfunctory praise he gives after Jenny has chosen to reject romance and freedom in favor of duty. His only response to her hesitant wondering if the Caddy really wanted her as a partner is the cynical, "Probably, baby. You're pretty well-equipped" (86).

In "The Last of the Wild Ones," collected in *Unicorn Variations*, Jenny has gone wild herself. Sam, although his revenge was completed with the destruction of the Caddy, continues to hunt the wild cars. His current vehicle, the Angel of Death, betters Jenny's machinery but lacks both Jenny's personality and her sense of sexual orientation. Although Sam thinks of this car as a "he," the fact that the car has a title rather than a personal name makes this a generic pronoun. Moreover, angels are fairly sexless creatures, so that when Jenny appears and insists on addressing the other car as "it" or "Whitey" rather than "he," the neuter pronoun only seems appropriate.

Sam clearly wishes to believe that Jenny's abandonment of him is merely the result of the virus program, but Jenny apparently feels otherwise: "you've spent the entire time [since her departure] hunting us. You had your revenge that day, but you kept right on – destroying" (41). Jenny's choosing to recall Sam's planned revenge reveals that her reason for choosing to kill the Caddy rather than going renegade at that point was based on empathy with Sam's need. When he continued his hunt after the Caddy's destruction, Jenny decides that Sam had lied to her and used her sympathies. The fact that she goes wild without killing Sam reveals that no random virus motivated her but that she escaped as a conscious protest. Only when Sam corners her at the end does she try and kill him, and even then she pauses to talk, as if he needs to know why she has behaved as she has. Through machines like Jenny and Maxine, Zelazny investigates the male desire for a perfect helpmate, a desire that seems to have its roots in the creation of Eve. Like Milton's Eve, however, when the female machine is treated too much as an accessory and too little as a person, the female may revolt – perhaps in order to assert that being female is not an excuse for being treated as less than a person.

In the novel *Roadmarks*, Zelazny presents two other female machines, the computer "books" Leaves of Grass and Flowers of Evil. The relationship between Leaves and Flowers and their male companions is less immediately that of creator and created than in the previous examples. Leaves and Flowers both have been the personal computers and assistants of Red Dorakeen. At the point where the novel begins, Flowers is Red's current companion. Leaves is in the nearly accidental possession of Red's son, Randy. When Red left Randy's mother (a casual relationship) "the only things he had left behind were his marked-up copy of *Leaves of Grass* and an embryonic Randy."[3] On reaching adulthood, Randy decides to go in search of his mysterious father and, when he accidentally stumbles on the code that awakens Leaves, she becomes his guide.

Leaves and Flowers are considerably more sophisticated than any of the female machines discussed thus far. As "microdot computers" they are both very small despite their power. They are also quite adaptable. At various times, in addition to their function as information brokers, the computers operate vehicles; detect magic, bombs, and smoke; and even become ultra-sonic weapons. Their sentience is apparent from the start as they advise, tease, and even argue with their human owners. Even the term "owner" is open to debate, for as a very indignant Leaves informs Randy:

> I evolve, I mature – the same as you do. I need not spend all my days as this sort of unit. I may have many adjuncts in my next avatar. I may command

complex operations of an extremely responsible nature. I might even be the
nervous system for a protoplasmic construct one day. (88)

Therefore, the nature of the relationship between Flowers,
Leaves, and their humans is closer to that of companions or trusted
employees rather than of servants.

Just as Zelazny makes clear that Leaves and Flowers are fully sentient beings, not tools, so he also provides opportunity to stress that
these computers perceive themselves not only as people but also,
despite the lack of anything vaguely resembling female shape, as female people. First, the computers speak with female voices and are
referred to by the feminine pronoun. Leaves makes an issue of this
when another character refers to her as "it": " 'I warrant a pronoun
these days,' Leaves said slowly and with a touch of menace, 'and it is
feminine' " (146). Later, Flowers jokingly threatens her passengers
that she will "gas you both permanently and become a Flying Dutchperson, like that car I heard about a while back, flitting down the
centuries with a pair of skeletons" (173). Flowers' deliberate choice
of "Dutchperson" rather than "Dutchman" reveals an awareness of
herself as not male that echoes now standard gender fair language
trends.

Another way that the computers demonstrate their femininity is
by openly exhibiting caring and emotional insight, both commonly
thought of as female traits. In the course of the story, Red tells Flowers that she is "more suspicious than half a dozen wives" (152), yet
the novel reveals that Flowers' intuition is correct, for Leaves believes that Red abandoned her when she became too concerned
about the same mysterious and suicidal behavior of which Flowers is
becoming aware. Flowers and Leaves also both react as females
when placed in sexually charged situations. Leaves' teasing warning
to Randy that if he travels to Carthage with Layla he'll "be into back
braces for a while" (147) reveals both a broad familiarity with human
sexuality not commonly thought of as part of being a computer and a
touch of rivalry between the two women. Flowers, although she remains loyal to Red, conducts an affair with Mondamay, a robot friend
of Red's whom they meet up with along the Road.

The final class of nonhuman woman in Zelazny's fiction is also
the one that bears the least resemblance to humanity. These are the
places that have been personified as female. There has long been a

tendency to personify certain places and things as female; boats are a particularly strong example of this. In "This Moment of the Storm," a short story collected in *The Doors of His Face, the Lamps of His Mouth*, Zelazny spends three paragraphs describing why the space station Beta Station became Betty. The final paragraph sums it up:

> she was what she was – a place of rest and repair, of surface-cooked meals and of new voices, new faces, of landscapes, weather, and natural light again, after that long haul through the big night, with its casting away of so much. She is not home, she is seldom destination, but she is like unto both. When you come upon light and warmth and music after darkness and cold silence, it is Woman. (173)

This charmingly sexist description of what makes a woman is hardly surprising in a story published in 1966. It says less about what a woman is than what American culture in the mid-1960s was still trying to believe a woman should be. Despite the fact that Betty's mayor is a woman, the setting of the story is still largely that of the time in which it was written. When the hero, Godfrey Justin Holmes, visits the mayor's office, the Mayor promptly makes coffee. During a lull in a major crisis, she takes time off to "prepare steaks, with baked potato, cooked corn, beer – everything I liked" (194) for Godfrey. When the crisis resumes, she weeps and collapses while he kills monsters and rescues victims. By the end of the story, the Mayor is a victim of the looters, and Godfrey, discovering that Betty is not the nice woman he imagined her to be, flees into space – presumably to find a nicer world.

In "This Mortal Mountain," first published in 1967 and reprinted in *The Doors of His Face, the Lamps of His Mouth*, again a piece of land is personified as female. This time the subject is an enormous mountain called the Gray Sister, a name that evokes the Gorgons of Greek mythology. The Gray Sister is described as "not a mountain. It is a world all by itself, which some dumb deity forgot to throw into orbit" (132). Of course, the protagonist, a legendary mountain climber named Jack Summers, decides to conquer the lady, speaking to her the night before the climb as if she can hear him and somehow understand his challenge and his desire. Jack, of course, manages to climb the Grey Sister, and, like a hero out of fairy-tale, awakens the ice-bound lady at the very top. Whether he has rescued his "princess" remains open at the end of the story, but as he explains to Linda, "Each mountain is a deity . . . If you make sacrifices on its slopes a mountain may grant you a certain grace, and for a time you will share this power" (170). Although the story ends with a hesitant prayer, the reader cannot help but feel that the Grey Sister will not deny her supplicant his duly earned reward.

"Permafrost," the Hugo winner for 1986, collected in *Frost and Fire*, also deals with a world that is female. In the case of Balfrost, the femininity is not merely personification. Once again, as in "This Mortal Mountain," the story presents a woman encased in ice, but unlike Linda, who is suspended, Glenda is quite alive through a symbiotic relationship with the permafrost that covers her. The permafrost functions as the nervous system for the living world, and she as its intelligence is able to effect changes in the world environment.

The story itself is one of those of embittered romance that appear so often in Zelazny's work. In this story, Glenda has the power of a planet with which to take her vengeance on Paul, the lover who abandoned her to die in an icy landslide. When they meet, she reanimates her dead body, forcing him into a grotesque embrace that seems emblematic of the desire for control that often motivates female sexual manipulations in more conventional stories. Glenda fails to destroy Paul only because of the intervention of the planetary computer's controlling intelligence, who will not permit her to take over the body of Paul's current girlfriend. The story ends with Paul's intelligence forced to trade places with the human intelligence that runs the world's defense and maintenance system. Now, able to match Glenda's ice with his own mechanical fire, Paul battles her throughout the seasons. The story's ending hints that this battle is what they both desire most: "the torment of love unsatisfied, or satisfied, in the frozen garden of our frozen world" (46). Unlike Godfrey, who fled Betty when she proved to be more dangerous than he had desired in a woman, Paul thrives in the stimulating challenge of a woman who wants nothing more than to destroy him.

Despite their secondary role in most stories, Zelazny's female characters are varied and often quite vividly developed. As his writing has progressed, he has mostly left behind the limited stereotypes that shaped so many of the female characters in his early works, replacing them with characterizations that focus on gender as an aspect of, not a replacement for, characterization. This development can be seen in the 1992 novelette "Come Back to the Killing Ground,

Alice, My Love." The sex of the clone "scarred Alice" is crucial to her role in the story, but more important is the vitality of intellect and will that enables her to challenge her maker, her allies, and even the destruction of her universe in order to win what she desires. Zclazny's development is also evident in the range of tactics, sexual and otherwise, used by the female characters to further their own aims in the later stories. No longer does the woman simply wait with hot coffee for the hero to save the day. Many of the female characters in the latter Zelazny stories seem quite capable of seizing the day for themselves.

Chapter Seven

What Next?

Autumn, late October 1992. Zelazny and I have met at the World Fantasy Convention, held this year in Georgia at Callaway Gardens. In between appointments and program items, we make our way across the road from the inn to investigate the varied wonders offered by the gardens – the butterfly house, the wild flower trail, the lakes.

On this particular day we have gone to visit the gothic meditation chapel, a stone building nestled between stream and lake and framed in sky and water by autumn foliage. As we walk back to the car, my attention is caught by a brilliant spot of orange suspended seemingly in midair. It is a spider, the fattest spider I have ever seen. She's so lovely, with her black and white stockings and her orange middle, that I call for Roger to come and look.

He walks back and studies her for a few moments before calling to my attention that she has just started spinning a web. Neither of us has ever seen a spider spin a web from start to finish so we stay to watch.

Our view of the web is perfect, backlit to show each strand, each motion of the eight furry legs. The spider starts from a rough center, extending her reach with long lines that resemble the spokes on a wheel, slowly stitching her way inward, tacking each tiny piece of near invisible thread with fluid from her abdomen. Although instinct may guide her choice of pattern, she is also sensitive to the minute shifts in tension in the threads. When a new force pulls against her growing construction, she places an extra line to balance it. Toward the top, where the pull is less, she frequently skips a round.

As she works, she gradually reduces in size, losing something of the incredible plumpness that had first caught my attention. Completing the web takes her about an hour, and when she settles in place at the web's center she is markedly weary.

Of course, there is a metaphor here, for Zelazny is a spinner of tales just as a spider is a spinner of webs. Like the spider, he has started from a personal center shaped by his parents and early education. From there he has extended outward, stretching his reach by educating himself with an almost instinctive awareness for what he will need. Like the spider, he is capable of adapting his original pattern to the pull of different forces. His most recent characters and stories are not the same as those he created 30 years ago. What he will create in the future will be different still.

I have no desire to push this metaphor too far, however. The spider we watched in Callaway Gardens completed her web in the hour we watched, and she was diminished by the process. Zelazny has spun many tales and, rather than diminishing him, the process seems to encourage him to continue spinning tales for the future, tales that will continue to ensnare readers with his unique vision of what is and what may be.

Notes

Chapter One

1. Roger Zelazny, letter to the author, 3 August 1989; hereafter personal letters will be cited in text as "letter."

2. Roger Zelazny, "Aikido Black" (unpublished essay, used by permission of the author), 5; hereafter cited in text.

3. Joseph Sanders, *Roger Zelazny: A Primary and Secondary Bibliography* (Boston: G. K. Hall & Co., 1980), xi; hereafter cited in text.

4. Roger Zelazny, personal interview, November 1990.

5. Samuel R. Delany, "Faust and Archimedes," in *The Jewel-Hinged Jaw: Notes on the Language of Science Fiction* (Elizabethtown, N.Y.: Dragon Press, 1977), 191-92; hereafter cited in text.

6. Roger Zelazny, *Creatures of Light and Darkness* (New York: Avon Books, 1970); hereafter cited in text as *Creatures*.

7. Samuel R. Delany, *We in Some Strange Power's Employ, Move on a Rigorous Line* (New York: Tom Doherty Associates, 1990), 19; hereafter cited in text.

8. Richard Cowper, "a rose is a rose is a rose . . . in search of roger zelazny," *Foundation: The Review of Science Fiction*, no. 11/12 (1977): 143; hereafter cited in text.

9. Joseph Sanders, "Zelazny: Unfinished Business" (Bowling Green, Ohio: Bowling Green University Popular Press, 1979).

10. Roger Zelazny, *The Last Defender of Camelot* (New York: Pocket Books, 1980), 1; hereafter cited in text as *Last Defender*.

11. Roger Zelazny, foreword to *Bridge of Ashes* (New York: Signet Books, 1976); hereafter cited in text as *Bridge*.

12. Roger Zelazny, "Introduction to 'For a Breath I Tarry' " in *A Very Large Array: New Mexico Science Fiction and Fantasy*, ed. Melinda M. Snodgrass (Albuquerque: University of New Mexico Press, 1987), 4; hereafter cited in text as *Array*.

13. A shared world is created when a group of authors write stories within a shared setting. Characters from different stories interact, and there is usually a consistent chronology. A mosaic novel uses a similar concept, but instead of a collection of discrete short stories the different authors' contributions are interwoven into a mosaic.

Chapter Two

1. Carl B. Yoke, *Roger Zelazny* (West Linn, Ore.: Starmont House, 1979), 13; hereafter cited in text.

2. Marcel Proust, *Within a Budding Grove*, trans. C. K. Scott Moncrieff (New York: Vintage Books, 1979), 159; hereafter cited in text.

3. Roger Zelazny, *Blood of Amber* (New York: Arbor House, 1986), 87; hereafter cited in text as *Blood*.

4. Roger Zelazny, "Roger Zelazny: Forever Amber," in *Locus* (Oakland, Calif.: Locus Publications, 1991), 68; hereafter cited in text as "Forever Amber."

5. Roger Zelazny, *Frost and Fire* (New York: William Morrow and Company, 1989), 281; hereafter cited in text as *Frost*.

6. Roger Zelazny, *The Chronicles of Amber*, 2 vols. (New York: Doubleday, 1978), 2:90; hereafter cited in text as *Chronicles*.

7. Henry Kuttner, *The Dark World* (New York: Ace Books, 1946), 20; hereafter cited in text.

8. Harlan Ellison, *Partners in Wonder* (New York: Walker and Co., 1971), 453; hereafter cited in text.

9. Roger Zelazny, "The Long Sleep," *Wild Cards XIII: Card Sharks* (Riverdale, N.Y.: Baen Books, 1993) 264-65; hereafter cited in text as "Long Sleep."

Chapter Three

1. Roger Zelazny, introduction to *The Illustrated Roger Zelazny*, ed. Byron Preiss (New York: Baronet Publishing Company, 1978).

2. Roger Zelazny and Neil Randall, *Roger Zelazny's Visual Guide to Castle Amber* (New York: Avon, 1988), 7; hereafter cited in text as *Visual Guide*.

3. Roger Zelazny, *Isle of the Dead* (New York: Ace Books, 1969), 28; hereafter cited in text as *Isle*.

4. Roger Zelazny, *Eye of Cat* (New York: Simon and Schuster, 1982), 155; hereafter cited in text as *Cat*.

5. Roger Zelazny, "Introduction" to "The Man Who Loved the Faoli" in *SF: Author's Choice 4* edited by Harry Harrison (New York: G. P. Putnam and Sons, 1974), 262; hereafter cited in text.

6. Roger Zelazny and Thomas T. Thomas, *The Mask of Loki* (New York: Simon and Schuster, 1990), 26; hereafter cited in text as *Loki*.

7. Roger Zelazny, liner notes to Bruce Dunlap, *About Home* (Cheskey Records, 1991).

8. Roger Zelazny, *Prince of Chaos* (New York: William Morrow, 1991), 85; hereafter cited in text as *Prince*.

9. Roger Zelazny, "This Moment of the Storm" in *The Doors of His Face, the Lamps of His Mouth and Other Stories* (New York: Avon Books, 1971), 189; hereafter cited in text as *Doors/Lamps*.

10. Roger Zelazny, *Sign of Chaos* (New York: Arbor House, 1987); hereafter cited in text as *Sign*.

11. Roger Zelazny, *Knight of Shadows* (New York: William Morrow, 1989), 159; hereafter cited in text as *Knight*.

Chapter Four

1. Theodore Sturgeon, in Roger Zelazny, *Four for Tomorrow* (New York: Ace Books, 1967), 7; hereafter cited in text as *Four*.

2. Roger Zelazny, *When Pussywillows Last in the Catyard Bloomed and Other Poems* (Carlton Victoria, Australia: Waratah Press, 1980), 1; hereafter cited in text as *Pussywillows*.

3. Roger Zelazny, *To Spin is Miracle Cat* (San Francisco: Underwood-Miller, 1981), 6; hereafter cited in text as *To Spin*.

4. Theodore Krulik, *Roger Zelazny* (New York: Ungar Publishing Company, 1986), 29; hereafter cited in text.

5. Roger Zelazny, *A Dark Travelling* (New York: Walker and Company, 1987), 81; hereafter cited in text as *Travelling*.

Chapter Five

1. Brian Aldiss with David Wingrove, *Trillion Year Spree: The History of Science Fiction* (New York: Atheneum, 1986), 294; hereafter cited in text.

2. Joseph Francavilla, "Promethean Bound: Heroes and Gods in Roger Zelazny's Science Fiction" in *The Transcendant Adventure: Studies of Religion in Science Fiction and Fantasy*, ed. Robert Reilly (Westport, Conn.: Greenwood Press, 1985); hereafter cited in text.

3. Roger Zelazny, *Unicorn Variations* (New York: Avon Books, 1983), 2; hereafter cited in text as *Unicorn*.

4. Joseph Francavilla, "These Immortals: An Alternative View of Immortality in Roger Zelazny's Science Fiction" in *Extrapolation* 25 (1984): 24; hereafter cited in text.

5. See my article, "All Roads *Do* Lead to Amber," *Extrapolation* 31 (Winter 1990): 326-32.

6. Roger Zelazny, *Lord of Light* (New York: Avon Books, 1967), 162; hereafter cited in text as *Lord*.

7. Roger Zelazny, *The Changing Land* (New York: Ballantine Books, 1981), 239; hereafter cited in text as *Land*.

8. Roger Zelazny, *This Immortal* (New York: Ace Books, 1966), 4; hereafter cited in text as *Immortal*.

9. Roger Zelazny, *Jack of Shadows* (New York: Signet Books, 1971), 177; hereafter cited in text as *Jack*.

10. In the introductory note to the novella "Damnation Alley" in the short-story collection *The Last Defender of Camelot*, Zelazny says: "I wrote the story. At my agent's suggestion, I later expanded it to book length. I like this version better than the book" (125).

11. Roger Zelazny, *Damnation Alley* (New York: Tor, 1984), 20; hereafter cited in text as *Damnation*.

12. Roger Zelazny, *Trumps of Doom* (New York: Arbor House, 1985), 84; hereafter cited in text as *Trumps*.

Chapter Six

1. Beverly Friend, "Virgin Territory: The Bonds and Boundaries of Women in Science Fiction." in *Many Futures, Many Worlds: Theme and Form in Science Fiction*, ed. Thomas D. Clareson (Ohio: Kent State University Press, 1977), 149; hereafter cited in text.

2. Roger Zelazny, *The Dream Master* (New York: Ace Books, 1966), 48; hereafter cited in text as *Dream*.

3. Roger Zelazny, *Roadmarks* (New York: Ballantine Books, 1979), 81.

Selected Bibliography

PRIMARY WORKS

Books

Blood of Amber. New York: Arbor House, 1986.
Bridge of Ashes. New York: Signet Books, 1976.
The Changing Land. New York: Ballantine Books: 1981.
Changeling. New York: Ace Books, 1980.
The Chronicles of Amber. 2 vols. New York: Doubleday, 1978.
Creatures of Light and Darkness. New York: Avon Books, 1970.
Damnation Alley. New York: Tor Books, 1969.
A Dark Travelling. New York: Avon Books, 1987.
Dilvish the Damned. New York: Ballantine Books, 1982.
The Doors of His Face, the Lamps of His Mouth. New York: Avon Books, 1971.
Doorways in the Sand. New York: Avon Books, 1976.
The Dream Master. New York: Ace Books, 1966.
Eye of Cat. New York: Timescape Books, 1982.
Four for Tomorrow. New York: Ace Books, 1967.
Frost and Fire. New York: William Morrow and Company, 1989.
Here There Be Dragons. Hampton Falls, N.H.: Donald M. Grant, 1992.
The Illustrated Roger Zelazny. New York: Byron Preiss Visual Publications, 1978.
Isle of the Dead. New York: Ace Books, 1969.
Jack of Shadows. New York: Signet Books, 1971.
Knight of Shadows. New York: William Morrow and Co., 1989.
The Last Defender of Camelot. New York: Pocket Books, 1980.
Lord of Light. New York: Avon Books, 1967.
Madwand. New York: Ace Books, 1981.
My Name is Legion. New York: Ballantine Books, 1976.
Prince of Chaos. New York: William Morrow and Co., 1991.
Roadmarks. New York: Ballantine Books, 1979.
Sign of Chaos. New York: Arbor House, 1987.
This Immortal. New York: Ace Books, 1966.

Today We Choose Faces. New York: Signet Books, 1973.

To Die in Italbar. New York: Daw Books, 1973.

To Spin Is Miracle Cat. San Francisco: Underwood/Miller, 1981.

Trumps of Doom. New York: Arbor House, 1985.

Unicorn Variations. New York: Avon Books, 1983.

Way Up High. Hampton Falls, N.H.: Donald M. Grant, 1992.

When Pussywillows Last in the Catyard Bloomed and Other Poems. Carlton Victoria, Australia: Nostrilla Press, 1980.

Collaborations

Dick, Philip K. *Deus Irae*. New York: Dell Books, 1976.

Randall, Neil. *Roger Zelazny's Visual Guide to Castle Amber*. New York: Avon Books, 1988.

Saberhagen, Fred. *Coils*. New York: Tor Books, 1982.

_____. *The Black Throne*. New York: Baen Books, 1990.

Sheckley, Robert. *Bring Me the Head of Prince Charming*. New York: Bantam Books, 1991.

_____. *If at Faust You Don't Succeed*. New York: Bantam Books, 1993.

Thomas, Thomas T. *Flare*. New York: Baen Books, 1992.

_____. *The Mask of Loki*. New York: Baen Books, 1990.

Unpublished and Miscellaneous Materials

"Aikido Black." Essay, 1990.

Liner notes to *About Home* by Bruce Dunlap. Cheskey Records, 1992.

"Two Traditions and Cyril Tourneur: An Examination of Morality and Humor Comedy Conventions in 'The Revenger's Tragedy.' " master's thesis, Columbia University, 1962.

SECONDARY WORKS

Books and Articles

Cowper, Richard. "a rose is a rose is a rose . . . in search of roger zelazny." *Foundation: The Review of Science Fiction* 11/12 (1977): 142-47.

Delany, Samuel R. "Faust and Archimedes." In his *The Jewel-Hinged Jaw: Notes on the Language of Science Fiction*, 191-210. Elizabethtown, N.Y.: Dragon Press, 1977.

Francavilla, Joseph V. "Promethean Bound: Heroes and Gods in Roger Zelazny's Science Fiction." In *The Transcendent Adventure: Studies of Religion in Science Fiction/Fantasy*, edited by Robert Reilly, 207-22. Westport, Conn: Greenwood Press, 1985.

_____. "These Immortals: An Alternative View of Immortality in Roger Zelazny's Science Fiction." *Extrapolation* 25 (Spring 1984): 20-33.

Fredericks, S. C. "Revivals of Ancient Mythology in Current Science Fiction and Fantasy." In *Many Futures, Many Worlds: Theme and Form in Science Fiction*, edited by Thomas D. Clareson, 50-65. Ohio: Kent State University Press, 1977.

Friend, Beverly. "Virgin Territory: The Bonds and Boundaries of Women in Science Fiction." In *Many Futures, Many Worlds: Theme and Form in Science Fiction*, edited by Thomas D. Clareson. Ohio: Kent State University Press, 1977.

Krulik, Theodore. *Roger Zelazny*. New York: Ungar, 1986.

Lindskold, Jane M. "All Roads *Do* Lead to Amber." *Extrapolation* 31 (Winter 1990): 326-32. Reprinted in *Amberzine* 2 (August 1992): 20-27.

_____. "Burn the Innocent." *Amberzine* 4 (August 1993): 14-20.

_____. "Starting Backwards." *Amberzine* 3 (March 1993): 22-26.

_____. "Zelazny's Santa Fe." *Amberzine* 1 (March 1992): 17-23.

Morrisey, Thomas J. "Zelazny: Mythmaker of Nuclear War." *Science Fiction Studies* 13 (1986): 182-92.

Rhodes, Carolyn. "Experiment as Heroic Quest in Zelazny's 'For a Breath I Tarry.' " In *The Scope of the Fantastic – Culture, Biography, Themes, Children's Literature: Selected Essays from the First International Conference on the Fantastic in Literature and Film*, edited by Robert A. Collins and Howard D. Pearce, 190-97. Westport, Conn.: Greenwood Press, 1985.

Sanders, Joseph. "Dancing on the Tightrope: Immortality in Roger Zelazny." In *Death and the Serpent: Immortality in Science Fiction and Fantasy*, edited by Carl B. Yoke and Donald M. Hassler, 135-43. Westport, Conn.: Greenwood Press, 1985.

_____. "Zelazny: Unfinished Business." In *Voices for the Future: Essays on Major Science Fiction Writers*, edited by Thomas Clareson, 180-96. Bowling Green, Ohio: Bowling Green University Popular Press, 1979.

Yoke, Carl B. "Roger Zelazny's Bold New Mythologies." In *Critical Encounters II: Writers and Themes in Science Fiction*, edited by Tom Staicar, 73-89. New York: Fredrick Ungar Publishing Co., 1982.

_____. *Roger Zelazny: Starmont Reader's Guide 2*. West Linn, Ore.: Starmont House, 1979.

_____. "What a Piece of Work Is Man: Mechanical Gods in the Fiction of Roger Zelazny." In *The Mechanical Gods: Machines in Science Fiction*, edited by Thomas P. Dunn and Richard D. Erlich, 63-74. Westport, Conn.: Greenwood Press, 1982.

Bibliographies

Levack, Daniel H. C. *Amber Dreams: A Roger Zelazny Bibliography*. San Francisco: Underwood/Miller, 1983.

Sanders, Joseph. *Roger Zelazny: A Primary and Secondary Bibliography*. Boston: G. K. Hall and Co., 1980.

Stephensen-Payne, Phil. *Roger Zelazny, Master of Amber: A Working Bibliography*. San Bernardo: Borgo Press, 1991.

Index

The Author

Jane M. Lindskold is assistant professor of English at Lynchburg College, in Virginia. She earned her bachelor's, master's, and Ph.D. in English from Fordham University in New York. During her first two years in graduate school, she held a Henry Luce Foundation Fellowship. During her second two, she held a Presidential Scholarship. Her academic publications include articles on Roger Zelazny, W. B. Yeats, and John Millington Synge. She has also published several short stories, including "Between Tomatoes and Snapdragons" in *Dragon Fantastic* and "Good Boy" in *Journeys from the Twilight Zone*, and a novel.

Twayne's World Authors Series

These recently published Twayne titles are available by mail. To order directly, return the coupon below to: Twayne Publishers, Att: LP, 866 Third Avenue, New York, N.Y. 10022, or call toll-free 1-800-323-7445 (9:00 A.M. to 9:00 P.M. EST).

Line	Quantity	ISBN	Author/Title	Price
1	_____	0805782907	Barbour/MICHAEL ONDAATJE	$22.95
2	_____	0805782982	Schuster/MARGUERITE DURAS	$22.95
3	_____	0805782826	Kelly/MEDIEVAL FRENCH ROMANCE	$24.95
4	_____	0805782737	Conroy/MONTESQUIEU REVISITED	$22.95
5	_____	0805782745	Bucknall/MARCEL PROUST REVISITED	$24.95
6	_____	0805782885	Talbot/STENDHAL REVISITED	$22.95
7	_____	0805782761	Falk/ELIAS CANETTI	$22.95
8	_____	0805782893	Tittler/MANUEL PUIG	$22.95
9	_____	0805782796	Wright/WOLE SOYINKA REVISITED	$22.95
10	_____	0805782818	Firda/PETER HANDKE	$22.95
11	_____	0805782680	Vickery/ALEXANDER PUSHKIN, REVISED EDITION	$22.95
12	_____	0805764240	Alexander/ISAAC BASHEVIS SINGER	$22.95

Sub-total _____

Please add postage and handling costs—$2.00 for the first book and 75¢ for each additional book _____

Sales tax—if applicable _____

TOTAL _____

	Lines	Units

Control No. [   ]   Ord. Type [SPCA] [   ]

__ Enclosed is my check/money order payble to Macmillan Publishing Company.

__ Bill my   ☐AMEX ☐MasterCard ☐Visa ☐Discover   Exp. date _____

Card # _____   Signature _____
Charge orders valid only with signature

Ship to: _____

_____

_____ Zip Code

For charge orders only:

Bill to: _____

_____

_____ Zip Code

For information regarding bulk purchases, please write to Managing Editor at the above address. Publisher's prices are subject to change without notice. Allow 4–6 weeks for delivery.   Promo # 78728 FC2615

Critical Essays Series on American Literature

These recently published Twayne titles are available by mail. To order directly, return the coupon below to: Twayne Publishers, Att: LP, 866 Third Avenue, New York, N.Y. 10022, or call toll-free 1-800-323-7445 (9:00 A.M. to 9:00 P.M. EST).

Line	Quantity	ISBN	Author/Title	Price
1	_____	0816173206	Scharnhorst, ed./ THE ADVENTURES OF TOM SAWYER	$42.00
2	_____	0816173168	Davis, ed./ ROBERT BLY	$42.00
3	_____	081617315X	Karpinsky, ed./ CHARLOTTE PERKINS GILMAN	$42.00
4	_____	0816173176	Burkholder, ed./ HERMAN MELVILLE'S *BENITO CERENO*	$42.00
5	_____	0816173184	Parker & Higgins, eds./ HERMAN MELVILLE'S *MOBY DICK*	$45.00
6	_____	0816173109	Thesing, ed./ EDNA ST. VINCENT MILLAY	$42.00
7	_____	0816173192	Gottesman, ed./ HENRY MILLER	$42.00
8	_____	081618884X	McKay, ed./ TONI MORRISON	$42.00
9	_____	0816173222	McAlexander, ed./ PETER TAYLOR	$42.00
10	_____	0816173087	Petry, ed./ ANNE TYLER	$42.00
11	_____	0816173095	Torsney, ed./ CONSTANCE FENIMORE WOOLSON	$42.00

Sub-total _____

Please add postage and handling costs—$2.00 for the first book and 75¢ for each additional book _____

Sales tax—if applicable _____

TOTAL _____

Lines   Units

Control No. [   ]   Ord. Type [SPCA] [   ] [   ]

___ Enclosed is my check/money order payble to Macmillan Publishing Company.

___ Bill my ☐ AMEX ☐ MasterCard ☐ Visa ☐ Discover   Exp. date _____

Card # _____   Signature _____
Charge orders valid only with signature

Ship to: _____

_____

_____ Zip Code

For charge orders only:

Bill to: _____

_____

_____ Zip Code

For information regarding bulk purchases, please write to Managing Editor at the above address. Publisher's prices are subject to change without notice. Allow 4–6 weeks for delivery.   Promo # 78720 FC2617

Twayne's English Authors Series

These recently published Twayne titles are available by mail. To order directly, return the coupon below to: Twayne Publishers, Att: LP, 866 Third Avenue, New York, N.Y. 10022, or call toll-free 1-800-323-7445 (9:00 A.M. to 9:00 P.M. EST).

Line	Quantity	ISBN	Author/Title	Price
1	_____	0805770143	Lauber/JANE AUSTEN	$21.95
2	_____	0805769129	Ben-Zvi/SAMUEL BECKETT	$21.95
3	_____	0805769366	Wagoner/AGATHA CHRISTIE	$21.95
4	_____	0805770194	West/ROALD DAHL	$21.95
5	_____	080576805X	Nelson/CHARLES DICKENS	$21.95
6	_____	0805769862	Weigel/LAWRENCE DURRELL, Revised Ed.	$21.95
7	_____	0805769773	Rosenberg & Stewart/IAN FLEMING	$21.95
8	_____	0805770305	Crane/RUTH PRAWER JHABVALA	$22.95
9	_____	0805770135	Beene/JOHN LE CARRE	$22.95
10	_____	0805770208	Pearlman/WILLIAM SHAKESPEARE: THE HISTORY PLAYS	$22.95
11	_____	0805770356	Hillman/WILLAM SHAKESPEARE: THE PROBLEM PLAYS	$22.95
12	_____	0805770321	Morrison/WILLIAM TREVOR	$22.95

Sub-total _____

Please add postage and handling costs—$2.00 for the first book and 75¢ for each additional book _____

Sales tax—if applicable _____

TOTAL _____

Control No. [_____]   Ord. Type [SPCA]   Lines Units [___][___]

__ Enclosed is my check/money order payble to Macmillan Publishing Company.

__ Bill my ☐AMEX ☐MasterCard ☐Visa ☐Discover   Exp. date _____

Card # _____ Signature _____
Charge orders valid only with signature

Ship to: _____

_____

_____ Zip Code

For charge orders only:

Bill to: _____

_____

_____ Zip Code

For information regarding bulk purchases, please write to Managing Editor at the above address. Publisher's prices are subject to change without notice. Allow 4–6 weeks for delivery.   Promo # 78723 FC2610

Twayne's United States Authors Series

These recently published Twayne titles are available by mail. To order directly, return the coupon below to: Twayne Publishers, Att: LP, 866 Third Avenue, New York, N.Y. 10022, or call toll-free 1-800-323-7445 (9:00 A.M. to 9:00 P.M. EST).

Line	Quantity	ISBN	Author/Title	Price
1	_____	0805739882	McKay/RACHEL CARSON	$21.95
2	_____	0805739661	Gerber/THEODORE DREISER REVISITED	$22.95
3	_____	0805739831	Fowler/NIKKI GIOVANNI	$21.95
4	_____	0805775331	Levernier & Stodola/THE INDIAN CAPTIVITY NARRATIVE 1550-1900	$22.95
5	_____	0805739874	Scholl/GARRISON KEILLOR	$23.95
6	_____	0805776419	Abramson/BERNARD MALAMUD REVISITED	$22.95
7	_____	0805740082	Leamon/HARRY MATHEWS	$22.95
8	_____	0805776435	Bales/KENNETH ROBERTS	$21.95
9	_____	0805764240	Alexander/ISAAC BASHEVIS SINGER	$22.95
10	_____	0805740066	Johnson/EDWARD STRATEMEYER AND THE STRATEMEYER SYNDICATE	$22.95
11	_____	0805776389	Baker/STUDS TERKEL	$22.95

Sub-total _____

Please add postage and handling costs—$2.00 for the first book and 75¢ for each additional book _____

Sales tax—if applicable _____

TOTAL _____

Control No. [   ]   Ord. Type [SPCA]   Lines [   ] Units [   ]

___ Enclosed is my check/money order payble to Macmillan Publishing Company.

___ Bill my   ☐AMEX ☐MasterCard ☐Visa ☐Discover   Exp. date _____

Card # _____   Signature _____
                                   Charge orders valid only with signature

Ship to: _____

_____

_____ Zip Code

For charge orders only:

Bill to: _____

_____

_____ Zip Code

For information regarding bulk purchases, please write to Managing Editor at the above address. Publisher's prices are subject to change without notice. Allow 4–6 weeks for delivery.   Promo # 78729 FC2616